MARIENAU

A DAUGHTER'S REFLECTIONS

ANNEMARIE ROEPER

KAREN MIREAU

for mother smith
with love
&
gratitude

♡

karen
mireau

Azalea Art Press
Berkeley, California

ISBN: 978-0-9849760-4-1

Front Cover:
Marienau School

Back Cover:
Photo of Annemarie Roeper
by Doug Elbinger Studios

To my children, grandchildren
and great grandchildren,
and future generations to come.

- *Annemarie Roeper*

To my parents
Richard and Cynthia Kozlowski
who have always believed in me.

- *Karen Mireau*

Marienau School

"I wonder how my children
will tell their story?"

- *Annemarie Roeper*

CONTENTS

CHAPTER ONE:
The End of Childhood

Lüneburg Heath

It was a picture perfect morning in Marienau. All around me, to the far horizon, fields of wheat were swept into one vast glowing sea. There was a warm autumn wind swelling over them, like a painter's brush, softly caressing my face, my auburn hair.

It seemed like a dream, or a photograph of a dream, as if I were one with the stark white clouds billowing up over the heath, the blue-upon-blue sky, the golden fields. And then there was the heather, a purple blanket spread out beneath the birch trees, stitching woods to fields. It was in glorious full bloom, as mesmerizing as a painting by Van Gogh.

The road to Marienau was made of trammeled earth. Deep, jagged ruts made it difficult to navigate by foot, worsened by the constant traffic of horses and buggies and the early autumn rains. There was a little sandy path on the side of the road and this was how I made my way from home to the village of Lüneburg. It was only a mile or so to the center of town—an easy walk for an energetic fifteen-year-old girl—but I had very sensitive feet. I wore sensible sturdy shoes, made for hiking.

I was going into the village alone, as I often did, to buy some books, just enjoying the pleasant sensation of the landscape and walking leisurely along the narrow path. I had been an avid bookworm since the age of four and once I'd learned to read, there was no stopping me. I had hungrily devoured all of the children's books we had that came from Norway and then started in on my Father's substantial library. He had many rare and interesting books, especially on art and art history. I read them all, from A-Z, and had started back again, rereading the passages that had first eluded my understanding.

Reaching the town church, I passed the grocery store and the barber's shop and made a beeline to the pharmacy, where they sold books in addition to medicines and herbs. I lingered there, browsing among the latest offerings and talking to the owners, whom I had known since early childhood.

My family often laughed about the time I had my hair cut out on the sidewalk in front of the pharmacy. I had long, heavy pigtails then, so by the time the barber was finished, there was a quite a pile of hair on either side of the chair. All of the neighboring merchants came to gape at me because they had never seen so much hair on one child's head. It used to take my nursemaid over an hour to braid it each day and my head would hurt from twisting and turning away from her strong, insistent hands.

Just down the road was the public school I had attended before becoming a student at Marienau. We had slates then instead of paper that we would write on with a stylus. To erase them, we would simply wipe them off with a cloth or, if the teacher wasn't looking, with a little spit and our sleeve. It was hard enough to write on a slate, but they forced me to write with my right hand when I was totally left-handed. My penmanship was the cause of much criticism among my teachers throughout my school life.

The public school was in an old building, always drafty and cold, and I didn't get along very well with the other children. The kids teased me because I lived in a big house outside the village. The girls were much more interested in the boys from our boarding school than in the village boys, who seemed coarse and uneducated in comparison with the wealthy sons of German gentry that attended Marienau. The village boys were quite jealous of this and I bore the brunt of this, too. Mostly, they avoided me, but that suited me just fine.

My only real friend in town was Margaret, the daughter of the pharmacist, who was quite well read. We shared a common love of books, and so we understood each other fairly well. At school, I was constantly sick with colds and flu. My parents finally removed me and allowed me to be tutored along with some other younger children at Marienau.

On my way home that day, I went back through the marketplace, hugging the three books I had purchased close to my chest. It was a peaceful, quiet afternoon in the village as I made my way over the cobble-stones. By now the sun had fully risen and it was quite warm. The street smelled strongly of horse dung. I was so excited about getting home and reading my new books that I narrowly avoided tripping over some pigs being herded across the square.

Although I wasn't religious, I had the sense that life had been very good to me in my fifteen years. Trouble had always seemed to pass me by and I had the feeling that all was right with the world.

As I neared the center of town, a loudspeaker was blaring. The unmistakable voice of Hitler was being broadcast on the radio. It was a terrible din, worse than any maelstrom. Suddenly, lots and lots of people had gathered, surrounding me, crushing me between them. The corners of my books dug into my skin so sharply that I could barely breathe. The crowd was now shouting loudly and thrusting their arms forward in response to the speech.

"Heil Hitler! Heil Hitler!" I could smell the acrid odor of their sweat. I was paralyzed. The energy in the crowd seemed to intensify, like a huge, hungry animal pulsing with hostility and menace.

The thought of joining in sickened me, but I was very aware at that moment that I was Jewish. Although I was a part of the crowd, I might be discovered and killed at any moment. It both shocked and titillated me—this powerful force surging through the bodies of the village people. A few of them I had known all my life and might look the other way if the opportunity arose; but there were others who would just as soon tear me to pieces. Did I lift my arm? I remember only clutching my books to me as if they alone could save me. I became invisible.

Somehow I managed to wrest free of the crowd. I walked slowly and deliberately back to the path to Marienau, terrified to turn around. I had always been a strange mixture of being very wise, but also very naive. I'd led a very protected life. No one had ever really been intentionally mean or hurtful towards me. But there I had been, all by myself, trapped in the middle of the Nazis. I wasn't equipped to deal with the taste of that kind of terror. The horror I felt was devastating.

As soon as the village was out of sight, I began to run, slowing down only once my lungs were burning. As I made my way back home, the fear followed me like a storm cloud turned bleak and ominous. My mind raced with dark questions and apprehension. In that moment, on that once perfect autumn day, my childhood officially ended.

CHAPTER TWO

Life at Marienau

The Road to Marienau

I ran up the spiraled stairway to my room two
steps at a time and flung myself on my bed. I was still in
shock. Everything gentle I had known had crumbled. To
have felt that kind of powerlessness was to know the
exploitation of every imaginable human weakness. It was
so clear to me that I had been surrounded by something
that was beyond evil. It was like a kind of death.

Somehow I composed myself, and then ran to class acting as if nothing had occurred.

Usually there was a ten-minute pause between classes. There was a place I would always go to near the radiator. I would stand there, warming myself, and the other students would gather around me and we would talk. This day was no different—I stood in my usual spot and chatted with the others, but I don't remember telling anyone what had happened to me.

After our usual coffee time that day, I went right back to my schoolwork. I really dreaded doing home-work. It was so boring! I wasn't a particularly good student. I never wanted to make an effort, but when I did I was outstanding, particularly in geometry. Despite my parents' radical educational methods and philosophy, the school curriculum at Marienau was in some ways very traditional—emphasizing reading, writing and, of course, arithmetic. That part of Marienau was mundane to me, which I suppose made me a very typical teenager. I sat in my room trying to do what I was supposed to do, but my mind kept snapping back to that terrible moment earlier in the day, replaying it over and over again until I was exhausted.

In the evening, it was my parents' custom to retire early to their bedroom. Some of the older students would come and say goodnight to them while they were already in bed. Not long before, my parents had received an official letter from the government warning them that it was inappropriate for a couple who was "Hebraic" to be so intimate with Aryan students. They continued the practice anyway because the students loved it, but this made it difficult to have private time with my parents. As a result, I never did tell anyone what had happened that day. It was such a shocking experience for me, that I completely buried the event.

In every aspect up until then, I had the most wonderful childhood, living in an ideal community and feeling very well protected and stimulated. There was always so much excitement at Marienau. So much music. So much art. So much love, honesty and friendship.

I lived in Marienau from the time I was ten until I graduated from high school at age eighteen. Even then I understood it to be the essence of my childhood. It still feels like an island of beauty filled with intellectual excitement and activity as well as the realization of ideal human relations. But the threatening clouds of Nazi Germany were on the horizon and, as it turned out, this was just the beginning of what would soon envelop us.

Classrooms at Marienau
(Side View)

**My Mother
As a Young Woman**

Without my Mother, I don't think I would have survived what was to befall us. My Mother was one of seven first female doctors in Vienna, Austria, although she never formally practiced. Later, she was analyzed by

11

Otto Rank and studied with Sigmund Freud to become a psychoanalyst. My Mother was a very committed Freudian and the whole idea of the unconscious was something that I absorbed as hungrily as my Mother's milk. I grew up with Freud as a very natural part of my daily life.

She was born Gertrud Wiener to Olga Lauer and Gustav Wiener[1], on October 7, 1889 in Prague, Czechoslovakia. My paternal Grandmother, Marie Lauer Bondy, was her sister. When my Mother and Father married, this made them first cousins. It was common during those days to be intermarried in that way and there was no stigma to it then. It was always on my mind, though, that the children of first cousins might turn out to be either idiots or geniuses. Although I don't think my brother and sister thought much about it, it haunted me all my life.

To illustrate my rather complex family tree a bit further, there was a similar relationship on the other side of the family. My paternal Grandfather's sister, Katerina Bondy, married David Lauer (who was no relation to the family). Their son, Paul Lauer, married my Mother's sister Mathilde. Their son, Max, who was later lost in the Holocaust, married Rosa Lauer (his cousin). This made our lineage confusing, but it was typical of those times.

I never met my paternal Grandmother, Marie Lauer Bondy, nor was I named after her; but I knew my maternal Grandmother Olga Weiner very well. Olga was white-haired when I met her. She had beautiful gray eyes like my Mother. Everyone's hair was long then and she wore it up in a bun. She was little compared to my Mother, who was a whole head taller than she was. She had a cozy house that we always loved to visit. It was near the railway station and looked down on a playground for children. Contrary to what you would do today, she had dishes of candy in every room. The result was that none of her grandchildren particularly craved sweets.

I never met Olga's first husband, Gustav Wiener[2], my maternal Grandfather, who died when he was rather young. Gustav was blind, as was his brother, and my Mother would tell me how the two brothers would sit together, never admitting to each other that they couldn't see. We were a very active family. Almost everyone in the family was an enthusiastic mountain climber. My Grandmother would take Gustav up the mountain and describe the landscape to him so well that he would come back and tell people exactly what he "saw."

My Mother really was a very beautiful woman and she made a point of being a lady. I think it disappointed my Mother deeply that her Father was never able to see how beautiful she was. She was always elegantly dressed and very, very popular within the school. When she was young, she always wore gloves, as was the custom, especially when you took a train ride, because everything was so dirty.

My Mother's large eyes were grey-green and shaped quite round. Her long hair was reddish-brown and very thick and heavy, like mine. She had it braided up somehow but she always had headaches because of her heavy hair. As a child, my Mother wore gold, ugly braces on her teeth—neither my Mother nor Father had good teeth. She was very tall for that era. I grew to 5' 6" and she was almost a head taller than I was. Her hands are what I remember most. They were quite beautiful. I loved my Mother's hands and actually I like my own hands, too, with long, graceful fingers like hers.

After the death of her husband, Olga and my Mother moved to Vienna. When my Mother turned seventeen, my Grandmother remarried a rather odd man named Rudolf Feldmann[3] and they moved to Hamburg. My Step-Grandfather was a wealthy lawyer who went to work for my Grandfather's bank. He had a silver cigarette case and in it were chocolate cigarettes. Each time a grandchild arrived he would offer us one in with a very grand and polite gesture.

He was a funny man. He had a huge handlebar moustache that he took tender care of. When he shaved, he had something that you put over your moustache and hung over your ears to smooth it down. I remember him singing opera in the loudest voice and at the same time brandishing his straight razor like a conductor in time to the music. I don't think anyone took him very seriously. He also had an unusual silver pocket watch and I often wondered what happened to it because it would not only tell the time, but the date and month and year. You can get those things today, but it was amazing then. It was probably very expensive.

It was well known in the family that my Grandmother Olga preferred my Mother's older sister, Mathilde (Matti), to her. When my cousin, Peter Lauer, was born just a few months before me, my Grandmother spent most of her time with him. I imagine that my Mother resented it, but my Mother was the more talented and brilliant sister in the family.

My Mother was always very adventurous and headstrong, particularly once she became a teenager, which may account for her conflict with her mother. At that time, girls had to be chaperoned at all times. Somehow she managed to get around this and it was rumored that when she was sixteen or seventeen she had a boyfriend who climbed into her bedroom each night.

My Mother also had a brother, Julius[4], who was born between my Mother and Mathilde. He was called

"Jula," rather a female-sounding name. Jula later became a very special friend of mine. As an adult, he became a successful businessman who imported Desitin Ointment, but at heart he was a poet and a very sensitive man.

My Grandmother Olga died in 1932, in her late sixties, shortly before Hitler came to power. We were glad she didn't experience that. I remember my Mother being very heartbroken by her own Mother's death. My parents were already running a school and she talked to everyone incessantly about her Mother then. Someone asked why she did that, because it irritated people. She said that that was her way of dealing with her grief.

My Mother was very highly educated—she knew five or six languages, and she played the piano beautifully. She couldn't decide whether to be a doctor or a concert pianist. She practiced her piano for six hours every day, taking great joy in playing for her Father. His death resulted in her losing her passion for music at that time. Soon after my Grandmother remarried, my Mother began to follow her dream of becoming a doctor. She put a lock on her grand piano so that she wouldn't be tempted to play it and began secretly studying at night because her Mother disapproved.

Later, my Mother was able to use her backgrounds in medicine and psychology to work with children. She was an excellent diagnostician. She was trained much differently than is done elsewhere. She relied a lot on her intuition—it was before they had the machines they have today—and I believe she saved many children's lives.

Everyone who met her fell in love with her. Her psychoanalytic background helped her a lot in being open and in understanding the complexities of relationships. She was especially popular and so wonderful with the children.

Each morning, I would sit near my Mother and have deep discussions with her while she was bathing. This sounds funny now, but it never felt unnatural or negative to me. It was part of our closeness and a good example of the freedom of spirit she embodied.

My Mother in Her Later Years

CHAPTER FOUR:
Early Memories

**My Mother
and Myself as an Infant
18 months**

My nickname growing up was "Maedi," meaning 'Little Girl.' Everyone knew me by this name. No one called me Annemarie until I was a grownup.

My Mother was completing her internship at the University hospital in Vienna while she was pregnant with me. She used to go to school on the streetcar.

One day all of a sudden she realized she was in labor. She got to the hospital on her own and with my God-mother Pauline Feldmann's help, I was born Annemarie Martha Bondy on August 27, 1918.

My Godmother was also my Mother's good friend. She was the niece of Rudolf Feldmann, my Step-Grandfather. Pauline was very petite and had dark hair and eyes. She was very Jewish looking in the sense of her facial features. She wore skirts and stockings and garters, like the women of that time. Pauline was one of the first women obstetricians. In those days women weren't doctors and that was unusual. Like my Mother, she went to medical school behind her parents' backs, as it was not acceptable during that time for women to study medicine. The first thing she did when becoming a doctor was to facilitate my birth.

**My Godmother
Pauline Feldmann**

When does memory start? I think my earliest memories would be just vagueness and maybe the warmth of my Mother's breast and being lost in it, but that must have been before consciousness. The first three months of my life I spent with my Mother as she was still studying then at the University of Vienna. She took me to the hospital with her every day.

Land	Wien
Behörde	Israelitische Kultusgemeinde
Nummer der Eintragung	1263/1918

GEBURTSURKUNDE

Familienname	Bondy ·x·
Vornamen	Annemarie ·x· ·x·
Zeitpunkt und Ort der Geburt	27. August 1918 ·x· Wien VIII., Langegasse 74 ·x·
Geschlecht	weiblich ·x·

VATER

Familienname	Bondy ·x·
Gemeinsamer Familienname	·x·
Vornamen	Max ·x· ·x·
Wohnort	Wien ·x· ·x·

MUTTER

Familienname	Bondy ·x·
Gemeinsamer Familienname	·x·
Vornamen	Gertrud ·x· ·x·
Wohnort	Wien ·x· ·x·

7 Mai 2002

(Tag der Ausstellung)

4a

**Birth Certificate
Annemarie Bondy**

I have a memory of lying on my stomach and seeing three blood spots in a triangle on my pillow. It was so very clear. I must have been able to count to three or realized the picture of this later. My Mother saw them one day and thought that the only reason there would be blood was that I might have lice. I had, indeed, been bitten. She then realized that there were lice all over the hospital and she didn't take me there any more.

Of course, what my Mother did at that time—to be working towards her medical degree and taking care of a baby at the same time—was highly unusual. Later, my Mother had a nurse take care of me; again, because she was working. One day, as my Mother happened to be walking through the park, she found me alone in my buggy screaming. She realized that the woman who was supposed to be taking care of me was somewhere in the bushes having a rendezvous with her boyfriend. She took me home and she used to tell me the story of how upset the poor woman was when she came back and couldn't find me.

I loved being in my Mother's arms. She treasured me, too, and I have to admit that I was always her favorite. She always smelled deliciously of a special eau de cologne—Blau-Gold Doppelt Blockegasse No. 4711 Eau—that has always been worn by the women in my family. The scent of this always reminds me of my Mother.

When I was born, my Mother had a lot of milk. She nursed me for two years and I was still nursing while I was walking. This was in opposition to the previous generation, who believed that if you were middle or upper class, you didn't nurse your own children. However, the food situation was very bad in Germany at that time; a whole lot of people were going hungry. Many women with extra milk would share it with others who had none. So, there was this other girl that she would nurse in addition to me. Later on this child came to our school. I really knew nothing about her, but I remember disliking her the moment I laid eyes on her. I just could

20

not stand that child and I think I told my Mother at some point, "I don't know why I don't like her!" She then told me the story of my sharing her milk with her. I think my Mother was right to tell me this, because knowing it made it sense. Her having so much milk made it possible for me to be a healthy child. But I still resented that girl.

Another one of my earliest conscious memories is when I was just about a year old. I must have run away from somewhere. I knew I was doing something I shouldn't, and I found myself near a river. Children would swim naked in the summer and until they were around ten years old, even girls would go topless in warm weather. There were some naked boys swimming there, and I think I knew they were boys so I imagine I stared at their penises.

That scene at the river must have impressed me a lot, because it is something that comes back to me quite often, but with no more details than I have just told you. I remember it just as if I was watching myself. I had very blonde, almost white hair then. I remember feeling guilty for staring at the boys but not much else from that very early period.

In 1921, when I was between three and four years old, my Mother sent me away to my Aunt Matti's house in Hamburg for three months while she was studying with and being analyzed by Dr. Otto Rank, the famous psychoanalyst who was also a protégé of Sigmund Freud. She was pregnant at that time and when I came back home on October 10, 1921, there was my baby sister, Ursula Babette Bondy[5] or "Ulla" as we called her, who had been born at home.

Even at the time, I couldn't forgive her for letting that happen. My place had been usurped without even an explanation. I imagine that my very terrible temper tantrums started then. I loved having tantrums and I have always thought they were good things because they show a child that they can have some power. You can scream and carry on and make things happen and no one can really stop you.

I was already known to be quite stubborn. One day while staying with Aunt Matti, she brought me with her while she did her shopping. In Germany at that time, in the suburb of Hamburg, people would go to the store and pick out what they were going to buy and then the store would deliver it. She took me along and on the way back, I had a major temper tantrum. For some reason, I sat down in the middle of a puddle and no one could move me. My Aunt asked a man who was coming by to wait there while she went home and got a baby buggy and then the man helped lift me into the buggy.

Sitting in that puddle was a wonderful thing. I remember feeling how wet it was. I really was a pretty bad little girl to do that, but I think it was a mistake of my Mother to make me go away just around the time the baby was born.

She was a good Mother, nevertheless. My Mother took good care of me and I learned so much from her! Every afternoon all the students would come and have tea with her and I would always sit right next to her. I would always try to have her talk to me instead of somebody else. I would get her attention by pulling her chin over to me—so much that she got a sore chin.

She was a very dynamic, yet gentle person. One of the things that impressed me the most, I think, was overhearing a teacher tell my Mother that she needed to protect me and take good care of me—that I was so sensitive and so different that there was no way of my becoming just like all the other children. My Mother went out of her way to do this. I have to thank her for this because she always treated me like an adult. She discussed almost everything with me and I felt very safe with her.

There was a situation when a little boy died at my parents' school. We were sandbox friends. I couldn't have been more than four or five at the time. After the students first heard about the boy's death they went wild—screaming and running around and to all eyes having a wonderful time. I was very shocked and angry, even though I was so young; that the reaction to the death of a child would be happiness, or at least that is the way it looked to me. My Mother explained it to me in psychological terms—that the children were happy to still be living and that also that it was a defense against the sadness and the experience of death. They were rejecting it, so to speak. But I couldn't identify with the reactions of the students. I remember at that time feeling proud that she could explain it to me and that I could understand it. I was able to look at it from a psychological point of view.

When I was five or six, I contracted Scarlet Fever. I was very, very sick and in bed for six weeks. I was so weak that when I first got up I fell down and had to learn how to walk again. My skin started to scale after having the illness and my nursemaid scolded me because she thought I had put bits of paper in my bed. Prior to this I had terrible ear infections. We didn't have heating pads back then, so they warmed up mashed potatoes and put them around my ears in a cloth. It felt good at first, but then it smelled terrible when it cooled down. Later, all of my cousins and I went to the doctor and had our tonsils "capped" or cut off. They did this in the doctor's office and then they sent us home a few hours later. There was no ice cream prescribed back then!

When my younger brother, Heinz Gustav Eric Bondy[6], was born on June 2, 1924, I was six years old. We were living then in Gandersheim. I remember being alone and standing outdoors by myself. Nobody paid any attention to me. I'm sure I resented it. My brother was a beautiful little boy. He had green eyes. He had blonde, curly hair down to his shoulders until he was six years old and my Father insisted he get a hair cut. My Mother didn't want to cut it. When he finally got his hair cut before going to school, he looked so different. I remember sitting next to him in the car, wondering who the boy next to me was. I didn't recognize him!

Around that time, our nursemaid, Babette, forced me to eat things I didn't like, especially meat. She threatened me by saying that the strange-looking tree outside the window would come alive and punish me if I didn't finish all my supper. I had developed a little trick where I could hide the food in my cheek so that it wasn't visible from the outside. Then I would make it to the bathroom and spit it all out. It gave me a sense of power because no one, not even Babette, could make me eat if I didn't want to. She also made me eat the same disgusting meal before bed—cream of wheat. There was some idea at the time that this was what children should eat in the evening, but it still makes me shudder to think of it.

I really did not like Babette. For one thing, my sister was named after her and I know that she liked Ulla better. Babette didn't like me either and one day she told me to cut her toenails. Of course being very young, I cut her and she slapped me, hard. She yelled at me, saying, "You are so clumsy!" This has stuck with me all my life. I still think I'm clumsy. I think she spanked me a lot, but my Mother didn't know it. Unlike other Germans at that time, my parents didn't believe in spanking or hitting children, although I know my Father punished me from time to time.

Once, when I didn't make my bed, Babette locked me in my room. But I had an escape route! I climbed out the window and up to a balcony, then slipped into another student's room and went on my way to class. I loved being able to outsmart her. That was always the basis of some security for me. Nevertheless, the memory of Babette was everywhere and I know I had nightmares about her. I would find myself turned around at the other end of the bed in the morning after tossing and turning all night. It was like I was fleeing from something or turning away from something bad.

One benefit of smartness is that you understand things and that you can think of alternatives. You can also fool people. You can take the cookie that was really meant for your brother or sister and things like that. I did this and felt quite guilty about it. I also felt a little guilty for hiding the food in my cheek and spitting it out, but also it made me feel good that I was so smart.

Despite this feeling, when I was little, I was pretty lonely. I can remember when I first realized that I was not like other children. I knew, of course, that everyone was different, but I felt so very puzzled. Why did other people react so differently from me? Why did they mistreat each other and things like that?

From the time I was born I seemed to have a heightened sensitivity to the world, beyond that of the people around me. The truth was, that despite feeling secure at Marienau, and later having the sense that I had a happy childhood, I was not a happy child. I was always reacting against something. I felt imposed upon and I felt it was almost as if I was fighting for my life. I felt that if I didn't have a strong hold over myself that I would die or be killed.

My overall impression while I was growing up

was that the world was an odd place, that I didn't fit in and that people didn't understand me. I was prone to a kind of depression that my Mother called the pain of the world or "Weltschmerz." I had a kind of cosmic dizziness, I think. Somehow sensing and unconsciously realizing things made me feel that I was just not normal.

Other things contributed to that feeling. I was left-handed and used the "wrong" hand. I was clumsy—I fell a lot—my knees were always bleeding. I also felt that I was not particularly pretty (my sister, in truth, was much prettier than I was). This may also have had to do with my Father's always telling my sister and I how beautiful my Mother was and that we could never compare to her.

Despite all this, the one thing that kept me grounded was my Mother. My Father was of equal importance, of course, but in an entirely different way.

CHAPTER FIVE:
Max Bondy

My Father as a Young Man

My Father didn't talk until he was three or four years old. They were concerned about his I.Q. Later he turned out to be one of the most gifted people I know. The reason he didn't talk was that he never got the attention he should have had because his siblings were born so close together.

He was born in Hamburg on May 11, 1892, the eldest son of Marie Lauer and Siegfried (Salomon) Bondy[7]. There were five children in the family. My Father, Max, was the eldest; his sister, Cornelia[8](or "Nelly" as we called her), was born ten months later in

1893; and barely a year after the twin boys, Curt and Walter arrived. Almost a decade later, another brother, Herbert "Fritz" Bondy[9], was born in 1902. My Grandmother died of pneumonia before I was born and my Grandfather never remarried.

**The Bondy Children:
Herbert ("Fritz"), Cornelia ("Nelly"),
Walter, Max and Curt**

In 1914 my Father had gone to serve as a volunteer artillery officer in the German Reichsheer in WWI. When I was born, the telegram sent to him was damaged somehow in transit. When my Father received it, it read: "Child Born/Mutilated." It wasn't until three months later that he learned that I was girl. He was one of those people who needed a son, and I know he wanted me to be a boy. Girls have penis envy anyway, so somehow that has stuck with me all my life. I think it took a long time before I accepted the fact that there was absolutely nothing I could do about being a girl. I felt all of this intensely, including that there were things boys were allowed to do that I wasn't. It just wasn't fair!

I used to try to walk like the boys, taking big giant steps. One time, just to show how fearless I was, I climbed up to the peak of the roof of the classrooms at Marienau. All the children cheered me on. It wasn't until I was up there that I realized that I didn't know how to get down. They had to lower me with a rope, but still I pretended that I wasn't at all afraid. For the most part, I did everything the boys did—at school and in my family I was surrounded by boys. My sister and I were the only girl cousins in the family, so it seemed natural that we had to keep up with them.

I know, also, that my Father was jealous of me. Since my Mother and he had never really lived together, he had no time to get used to marriage before there was a child. He really didn't care for me very much when I was an infant. One story was that he tried to stick me in a wastebasket in order to keep me safely out of the way. It was a joke, of course, but a telling joke. Another story my Mother told me was that due to the beginnings of the recession then, there was hardly anything to be bought. The only thing she could put me in when she was traveling outside of Vienna was a suitcase. She was always afraid that someone would not see me and close the top on me.

My parents had always known each other. Since they were first cousins, they grew up together. Even though they lived in different cities, they saw each other often at family gatherings and on family vacations.

During the summer of 1912, I know that they traveled to Italy together with their families. It was then that they grew even closer. I never heard any details anything about their wedding other than it was a bittersweet time. They were married in Hamburg on September 30,

1916 while my Father was home on furlough. His Mother, Marie Lauer Bondy, had been ill and died shortly after. While they were on their honeymoon they learned that Max's brother, Walter, was killed by friendly fire in WWI and so they returned early and my Father went right back to the front. A year later my Father recieved the Hanseatenkreuz (Hamburg Medal of Honor) for his own service in the war.

I don't know that my parents ever fell in love; it just kind of fell into place for them. I think they loved each other very much, although they both had attractions to others. This was partially the times, and partially because they were both very charismatic people. It was a free, somewhat bohemian time. They were affectionate towards each other, and sometimes in the morning they would lock the door to their bedroom, which probably meant that they were doing something.

I loved in the morning to come into their bed (they had two beds put together) and lie between them on top of the boards that separated the beds. My parents always had breakfast in bed and I always got the tip of my Mother's boiled egg. I probably got more to eat than that, but that was the first thing I got in the morning.

Even when he was a child, my Father was very handsome. He had a kind of an aristocratic face. He was proud of not looking Jewish, and he didn't have any features normally associated with being a Jew. He was fiercely committed to his German identity, rather than German-Jewish culture.

My Father was rather tall and slim, like me, and very well built. He was very vain about his hair. Later in life he would comb long strands of it over the bald spot on his head. He had a sense of humor about it. He had a name for each strand. Women were just crazy about him and he was crazy about women—just as my Mother was crazy about men. There was a totally different attitude about relationships then and theirs was what we might consider today to be a rather unorthodox marriage.

My Father in Middle Age

As a child I had terrible fears and anxieties every night at bedtime. I was just so afraid of dying and of all the horrible things I knew were happening in the world. That was the one time my Father would pay attention to me. He would sit next to me on my bed and hold my hand. I don't quite remember what he said to me but it must have been things that made it possible for me to go to sleep.

Of course, he was everything in my life. It was not really an ideal situation for me because he was the head of our school. He was extremely beloved by every one of his students, so his attention was always on them. I think in other schools often the students criticized their leaders and found ways of working against them, but that wasn't the case at Marienau. At Marienau, there was nothing but my Father (and my Mother of course, too), but they were a kind of unit and the creators of my world and so for me, he was God.

I wanted nothing more than to be close to him. It wasn't until I turned fifteen that my Father realized that he had a pretty bright daughter who understood his philosophy. I was very much like he was. In some ways, I might be even more like him than he was himself. I feel that I kind of inherited his soul.

He was prone to depression his entire life. I remember once at Marienau seeing him enter the room with a face so completely crestfallen that it disrupted all conversation. His sadness could be so penetrating. My brother saw it as his task to amuse my Father and to keep him from falling into depression. My Father used to say Heinz was his one joy—and that playing with him always made him feel better.

He had a wonderful sense of humor and the students simply adored him. We were always laughing. He was witty and funny and when he was in a good mood, you could feel the whole atmosphere change. He played the piano very well and one of his favorite activities was for students to stand around him, singing the folk songs that he was playing.

Like my Mother, he was also very highly educated, especially in art history, which was his passion. He had spent much time in Italy and had seen every piece of art there first hand. In August of 1910, he graduated from the Wilhelm High School in Hamburg. When he began studies at Munich University in law and economics in 1910/11, he changed his major to art history, continuing his studies at Erlangen University and utilizing his winter term to tour Italy and deepen his knowledge of art. At age twenty, while studying art and history at Freiburg University, he published a treatise of his humanistic educational philosophies, *Die Grundlagen der Freischaridee* (The New View of the World in Education). He completed his Ph.D. in Art History in December of 1919, the year after I was born, when my Mother and Father were reunited in Erlangen. His dissertation was titled *Baiersdorf, eine kunstgeschichtliche Untersuchung* (Baiersdorf: An Art Historical Study.)

My Mother and Father traveled together all through Italy long before they were married, which was very unusual at the time. Later, he would take us and usually some other students through Italy and show us everything that he knew. We probably got the best education in art that anyone could get. My Father knew every gargoyle in Europe and could describe how they were different. He knew all the different architectural styles. The Gothic style was his favorite and I don't know how many churches we visited. The most famous one was the Dom in Cologne.

I just ate it up when we were on vacation together. It was the only time we really were together as a family. When we were traveling, I would sit in the back seat, feeling a bit frightened that the wheels would come off the car. I knew that it was silly, though, and I never told anyone.

I must admit that it was hard to share my Father with so many people. My Mother made it worse by saying, "You have to share us with these other children, who don't have their parents." This made me think that maybe I should really relinquish him to them in some way. Of course I was used to sharing him, but we never had a typical family life. Only on vacation would we sit at a table as a family. I think that I missed that and that I never had the experience of being seen as special by my Father. Neither did my sister. It was my brother, Heinz, who was really the apple of his eye.

**My Father Max
and My Brother Heinz**

Origins

Marienau Front Entrance
(My Room at Center Window)

Before Marienau became my parents' school, it was called "Hungerdorf" or "Hunger Village." The name really arose from the soil it was built on, which was not productive for the growth of fruit and vegetables. It was mostly sand, rather flat, and probably in itself had nothing compelling about it; but it created its own unique beauty by the wide-open spaces, which were

35

covered for miles and miles with the autumn heather I loved so much. Someone (who, I don't know) had named the farm Marienau before our time.

It was crisscrossed with small country roads where the Heidschnuke, or moorland sheep, and the brown and white cows would wander around randomly. The cows would 'moo' loudly and scare the children. Old farms, some hundreds-of-years old, were scattered around the landscape and many of the people kept beehives and made "Heide Honig" or heather honey, which is still highly prized for its strong taste and unusual texture. To me, heather honey is the very best honey in the world.

Somehow in the middle of all this, was the farm called Marienau, which was a rather big piece of property stretching over 300 acres that my paternal Grandfather gave to my Father as his early inheritance. It originally consisted of one main building—a white stucco farmhouse with a red-tiled roof—where my family and some of the students lived. Later, the surrounding stables were converted into classrooms, dormitories and single rooms for the students by architects Oskar and Hans Gerson[10].

It was there, at Marienau, that my parents continued to develop their idealistic school community and boarding school. Most of the students came from rather wealthy families who lived in Hamburg, about forty miles away. It seems to me that a number of them were from broken homes.

There existed different schools in Germany at that time. Children from the same family would go to specialized schools, probably from fourth grade on. If they were interested in music, they would go to music school; if they were interested in science, they would pursue that. These were public schools.

36

Then there were the private boarding schools, like Marienau, which were separate. There were many of them, some which were very innovative. Each had a different philosophy or point of view, often overlapping. Some were more philosophical, some were more practical, but each took itself very seriously.

There were many conservative rural boarding schools (Landerziehungsheime) and free schools (Freie Schule) at that time. Marienau was not the most radical, but it definitely was one of the most liberal, progressive and most intellectual, with a philosophy based on social responsibility and the ideal of making the world a better place.

The best-known school at the time that followed the idea of radical reform was one called "Salem." It was different from the other private schools because it was founded by gentry, the people who were titled or with special status, usually with a "von" or a "graf" in their name.

There was another school named "School of the Ocean" that existed on an island in the North Sea, run by a very interesting, romantic old fisherman. He taught his students sailing and crabbing on the islands nearby. It was very interesting because the school had no sports fields. When there was low tide, there would be a natural field on the beach for the students to play on and all sports would take place before the tide came back in.

When I was twelve, I went there myself for three months as an exchange student. I was supposed to stay for a year, but I was unhappy—they believed in "hardening" you—you had to sleep on a thin mattress on a hard board and when you went to the bathroom you had to go to an outhouse in the middle of the night. I came home after summer vacation. Shortly after that, I had my appendix out, so I never went back. The other exchange student stayed with us for the entire term where we had nice, comfortable feather beds.

My parents' school had existed in several other places before it was moved to Marienau on Easter of 1929. A school had originally been planned with a group of my Father's friends. Some of them, who happened to be in his artillery unit, were tragically killed while my Father was on leave in Vienna after I was born. So my Mother, Father and several friends, including Harald Schultz-Hencke and Martha Paul-Hasselblatt, founded the "Freie Volkschochschule" or Free High School in 1919. My Grandfather purchased a former hotel called Sintalhof where the school was then housed.

In 1920/21, they founded the "Freie Schule und Werkgemeinschaft" (Free School and Work Community) in Brückenau, where my sister Ulla was born. Brückenau was quite a bit south of Hamburg in the middle of Germany, and was famous for their brine spa where people came and took mud baths. This was considered a very elegant thing to do back then.

My parents rented a building from a next-door neighbor, Dr. Brunotte, an unusual man who kept a lot of birds that flew about freely inside his house. It seems to me that there were not more than thirty or forty students at Brückenau, mostly boys, because boarding schools could not be coeducational at that time. There were a few girls in addition to my sister and myself, and the girls always had to "disappear" on a hike or something when there was an inspection by the government. The Free School was co-founded with Ernst Putz, who later became a member of the Reichstag parliament. My parents' philosophies differed from his to the extent that several years later, they parted ways.

In 1923 my parents moved the school to Gandersheim, more in the southern part of Germany, which was also known for its mineral springs. There they rented a former sanatorium and founded "Schulgemeind Gandersheim" (School Community Gandersheim.)

Schulgemeind Gandersheim
(School Community Gandersheim)

Gandersheim was a historic town with cobble-stone streets dating back to 856 near a river lined with weeping willows. Every evening we would go to the Gander River Promenade and people would dress up and walk about. In the center of the square there was a big rotunda. Often an orchestra playing "oompah-pah" music or some other form of entertainment would be performing there. There were always tables where you could sit and eat pastries and have cake and coffee.

We lived up a steep hill from the classrooms in an ivy-covered building with a nice garden called "The Brown House." I had a scooter then and I would go really fast down the hill. I loved that scooter and I was heartbroken when someone stole it, which led me to do something I have always regretted. I took advantage of being my parents' daughter and told a lie, blaming the theft on a girl at my parents' school, even though I knew she hadn't done it. They believed me and not her and I vowed never to take advantage of my special status at the school ever again.

Gandersheim Abbey

I clearly remember the twin spires of the stone Lutheran Church of Gandersheim Abbey. Built in the tenth century in the Gothic style, it always seemed to dominate the small village. This particular church was renowned for its abbess, Saint Hrozwita or Roswitha, known as "The Nightingale of Gandersheim." She was a highly accomplished woman and a noted poet of that time. I believe she may have been one of Germany's first female writers.

One of my best memories of Gandersheim is the

sound of the train that passed by my window early each morning. The percussion of a train still sounds like music to me and instantly brings me back to those days.

My Mother described our move to Gandersheim as a very difficult time. Although her Father-in-Law was providing the means for them to make the move, German inflation made it difficult to obtain food and supplies. By enrolling students from other European countries who paid in foreign currency, they were able to support the school. It was there that they began implementing Sigmund Freud's ideas—a bold undertaking since Freud was not at all popular at that time, and the school became co-educational. Theater, music and dancing as well as lively philosophical discussions at Gandersheim were a precursor to life at Marienau.

In keeping with the school philosophy of communal participation in all matters, when it came time to decide to move the school, the students had a hand in choosing the location. They bicycled the thirty-five or so miles from Hamburg to Marienau and only when they gave their approval did my Grandfather purchase the property in 1928. We moved to Marienau once the remodeling on the main building was completed in 1929.

Every morning at Marienau began with a lovely Bach concerto played on my Mother's particularly good Bechstein grand piano. There was a walkway in the main part of the house on the second floor where my family lived and where my Father had his office, with a spiral stairway leading down to the foyer. Like a beautiful dream, the music would float up the stairway to my bedroom where I could hear it as I awoke.

I had my own room at Marienau, while my younger siblings Ulla and Heinz shared a bedroom. They got along much better than my sister and I did. We were so close in age that we were always competing. There was also a room near ours for our nursemaid, Babette.

Ulla and I were about the same size. When we were young, we really didn't play much together. Ulla was exceptionally pretty and I felt that everyone liked

**Ulla Bondy, Age 3
and Annemarie, Age 6**

her better than they liked me. She had beautiful brown hair with a red tint to you, like mine, and the most beautiful blue eyes. They were very striking and brilliant. I was probably jealous of them. She was a very playful person and very active. She was more gregarious than I was. I was a dreamer—unless I became overcome with something, and then I would talk and talk and talk.

The rivalry between my sister and I always seemed to escalate on trips because we would be so close together then. Once she locked me, naked, onto a balcony in the middle of an Italian town. Now it seems funny to me, but at the time I was just grief stricken.

She was one of those people who walked in their sleep. She would wander the house and my Mother would warn everyone to be sure and bring her back to her room if they found her. One night when I was asleep, I woke up with her foot on my chest and her arms spread wide apart with her shouting, "I am the victor! I am the winner!" She was fast asleep!

Despite being competitors, I loved my sister very much. My brother Heinz and I were always very close. Our life at Marienau became a bond that could never be broken.

Siegfried Bondy and Max Bondy

To understand Marienau completely, you must also know something about my Grandfather, Siegfried (Salomon) Bondy, and the history of the Bondy family.

A very clever businessman, my Grandfather grew quite wealthy by importing sugar from Brazil and investments in the banking business. His Father, Leopold, and

45

his Mother, Anna, had owned a small bakery in Bohemia, so there was a saying in the family: "from baking to banking." My Grandfather changed his name from Salomon to Siegfried, because he thought it was better for business. From his very modest beginnings, he became a millionaire. When I knew him, he had a cook, several chambermaids and a chauffeur named Mr. Buk, who had been in the service of the family for many years and was later retrained from driving a horse-drawn coach to driving my Grandfather's car.

My Grandfather was one of the first people in Germany to own an automobile. It was a 1931 Full Classic Series 90 Buick Limousine, which was an especially elegant car. It held seven passengers and weighed more than 4000 pounds and cost over $2000—a small fortune at that time. It had a horn on the outside. When he arrived at his house, a crowd would always gather

**Example of My Grandfather's
1931 Buick Limousine**

because in those days it was so rare to see a car, much less one as impressive as that. The car was very shiny and black and it had windows made of plastic, not glass. You had to get out of the car and put a bar into the crankshaft and turn it to get it started. The interior seats were covered in soft cloth and it had a gearshift on the inside. I rode in it many times. There was a door between the chauffeur, Mr. Buk, and the people sitting in the back. If you wanted to talk to Mr. Buk, you had to slide the window over to speak to him. Prior to that we traveled by horse and buggy. Once, my brother Heinz fell out of the carriage and almost hit his head upon a stone.

Like my Grandfather, my Father was passionate about automobiles. He loved to drive. One day, my Mother was riding in the car while my Father was driving and somehow the plastic windows caught on fire. It looked as though the car would explode but as it happened a fire engine was passing by and put out the fire.

My Grandfather was an average-looking man, with no hair at the time I knew him. He didn't have beautiful hands like my Mother—his fingers were quite short and stubby. He usually wore suits and long-sleeved shirts with a bowtie and a stiff collar. I was always thinking the collar would be painful, but maybe it wasn't. My name for him was "Gross Papa" (Big Daddy.)

Although he could be very generous, my Grandfather was well known to be a miser. One day he took me to the cemetery to look at my Grandmother's grave. He began to argue with the gardener about what he was charging, trying to get him to charge one mark less. This was so embarrassing to me. I thought it was terrible that he was arguing about it.

I remember there was a very popular restaurant in Hamburg called Jacob's. It was a lovely place on the water and our whole family met there for dinner from time to time. My Grandfather took me aside one time and confided, "Now, watch this. They are going to expect me to pay for it all." And it was true. They did. And he did. We were good friends. He told me, "You are the only person who likes me for who I am and not for my money."

As you might imagine, my father and his siblings grew up in a very privileged environment. In 1907 my Grandfather commissioned the building of a huge art-nouveau villa. Known as "The Bondy House," which still exists at Jungmannstraße 3 in Hamburg, it became a favorite meeting place for many of the famous artists

ABB. 13. WOHNHAUS S. BONDY, ALTONA-OTHMARSCHEN, 1907.
AUSSICHT VOM GARTEN, SÜDSEITE

ABB. 14. WOHNHAUS S. BONDY,
ALTONA-OTHMARSCHEN, 1907

Bondy House / Exterior / 1907

and intellectuals of the day. He also built a house next door at Jungmannstraße 1 for his daughter, Nelly, when she married.

Hans and Oskar Gerson, the young architects who built my Grandfather's house, were very well known in Europe for their elegant, modern buildings in the style of Brick Expressionism, which used ranges of colors and types of brick in patterns as well as angular elements in their design. You can see this in photos of my Grandfather's house as well as in the buildings at Marienau that they converted.

The Gersons built a residence for themselves near my Grandfather's villa that had two mirrored wings that housed each of their families. It had a very beautiful

Bondy House / Courtyard Fountain

garden. I spent a lot of time there as a child. They were very close friends of my family, especially the children. Many years later I came back to Hamburg and there was an exhibit about The Bondy House. I was looking at the exhibit when a young man standing next to me said, "What a beautiful special place that was." I told him it was my Grandfather's house. He was an architect studying German architecture and he told me how famous the house was when it was built, and now.

Some of my best memories took place at my Grandfather's, where we always spent our summer vacations. It was really a mansion that had running water and electric lights, except for the cook's apartment, which remained gas lit. It was one of the first homes in Hamburg to have electricity. It was a very rich household by any standard. There was a big dining room and a maid serving the food. My Grandfather also had a butler. At breakfast, people would come when they wanted, but at lunch we would all sit at the big table. We would all be talking at once. There was usually an extra table just for the children.

The house had a tennis court and a bicycle path around the orchard, which was planted with all sorts of things—apples and pears and cherries. There was a fountain in the courtyard and in the middle of the courtyard was a statue made in the image of my youngest Uncle, Herbert "Fritz" Bondy, whose nickname was "Daddy" (no relation to the American term for Father.) We played 'Cowboys and Indians' in the orchard. Once, we put on a play in which I was the Princess being caught by the Indians. They tied me very strongly to a tree and then the 'Cowboys' saved me. I vividly remember being tied to that tree! My Uncle Daddy made a home movie of this on that day.

My "Uncle Daddy"
Herbert "Fritz" Bondy

We did a lot of bicycling and playing tennis at my Grandfather's. The boys used to sit on top of an overpass where the cars would be going by underneath. The boys would spend hours and hours writing down the license plates of the cars passing under the bridge and if they found a duplicate, they would get all excited. I was bored to death by this, because I couldn't care less about license plates, but that was the one thing they liked to do best, besides playing field hockey, and generally we did what the boys did. I don't remember playing with dolls at all, but we played croquet endlessly. We also played a game called Bocha—throwing a ball and hitting it. I liked playing that.

The children who stayed at the house were all boys except for my sister Ulla and I, and of course they had to find out what a girl looked like. We all did a lot of looking and we got scolded for it. I don't think that bothered me particularly. I was more excited about being such a sensation. I thought it made me special. Otherwise, I was always taught that girls had penis envy. The Gerson girls, the daughters of the architects who built my Grandfather's house, were probably there with us. We were very friendly with them.

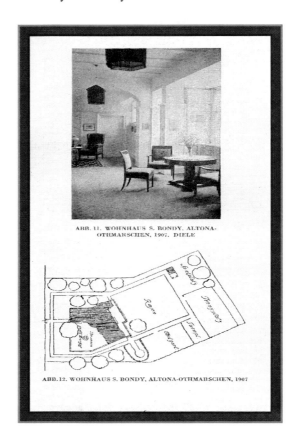

ABB. 11. WOHNHAUS S. BONDY, ALTONA-
OTHMARSCHEN, 1907. DIELE

ABB. 12. WOHNHAUS S. BONDY, ALTONA-OTHMARSCHEN, 1907

Bondy House / Interior

There were many bedrooms in the house. My Grandfather's room had a bed on a platform. You had to go up a little stepladder to get into it. There were a number of rooms we would stay in as children. My brother almost fell out a window one time, but I pulled him back at the last minute. He must have been a toddler, as I was about nine at the time.

My Uncle Curt had an apartment in that house, on one end of it. He lived with my Grandfather long after the rest of the children had gone. There was a big green billiard table at the end of the big hallway in a separate room with a little tally at the edge of the table to keep track. All the men played billiards, but we children loved to play, too.

My Grandfather's Czechoslovakian cook, Josephine Kaderabek, was a funny woman. She didn't know how to read or write, but she didn't want to admit it. Once she was listening to the radio telling a story and I saw her sitting with a book upside-down in her hand,

**The Bondy Cook
Josephine Kaderabek**

pretending to follow along and appear to be reading. She was afraid of electricity, so her apartment in my Grandfather's house had gas installed instead. Everybody loved Josephine. My Uncle called her, with great affection, "The Witch" because she looked a little bit like one.

My cousin George, who wanted to become a doctor, was always interested in dissecting things. One day he brought her the head of a dog and he wanted her to help him dissect it. I remember seeing him bring the dog's head in and her being very disgusted with it.

The suburb where my family lived was called Gross-Flottbeck. It was like a little village with all my relatives living there. The town next to that was named Blankenese and all of that was near the Elbe River. It was a major European port and a very lively, active river. We would sit at Jacob's Restaurant and watch the large boats go by, hear the horns tooting and see the rowboats, barges of containers and sailboats floating by. We often went on river trips.

My Cousin
Jan Gerhardt "Gerdi" Wiener

Our neighbors were the four Duschenes boys, the children of the daughter of my Grandfather's house-keeper, Frau Winsemann. They lived on the next street over from my Aunt Matti's house. My Mother's brother, Jula, lived just a few streets away from them. My cousin, Gerdi (Jan Gerhardt Wiener)[11], who was two years older than I was, grew up to be an adventurer who lived an amazing life. As a child, Gerdi used to tease me to no end. He and his older brother Thomas[12], whom we called "Chum," had a big dog and Gerdi would get that dog to chase after me, trying to scare me. Otherwise, it was very pleasant.

When I tired of being at my Grandfather's house, I would go to live with my Aunt Matti. She married Paul Lauer in 1905 and they had two sons, George and Peter. Peter Lauer[13] was three months younger than I, while George Lauer[14] was eleven years older. Both of them had brilliant red hair and grew to be so tall that you could never lose them in a crowd. They were really quite a family and all of them had a good sense of humor. My Uncle Paul would sometimes organize spitting contests to see who would spit the furthest.

My Aunt Matti's house was also designed by the Gerson brothers. It was a much smaller house. It had a living room and a dining room and several bathrooms. In those days, it was not so common to have indoor plumbing. I have a feeling that I shared a bedroom with my cousin Peter when I was there since we were so close in age. There was another bedroom for my cousin George, one for my Aunt and Uncle, and a guest room. Up in the attic were two rooms for the maids and another for their cook.

My cousin Peter was always full of games. He played marbles a lot. The foot of my Aunt and Uncle's bed could be lifted up and the bedrail had grooves that marbles could run down. He could do this for hours. But that was just one of his diversions. The whole house was covered with his electric train tracks. You couldn't really walk anywhere because the track was everywhere, except on the stairs.

My Cousin
George Gustav Lauer
and Family

There was another big piece of property my Grandfather owned that we called, "Lurup." That property was right next door to the Hamburg airport and later on incorporated into the airport. It became enormously valuable later on.

Later on, when I was about fourteen, my Grandfather was run over by a streetcar. I visited him at home then, but he had a long catheter and when I saw that, I broke into tears. I thought it was so sad for this strong man that I used to know to be in such a state. I didn't want him to see that I was crying. He finally died of his injuries and was cremated. He didn't want to be buried in the Jewish cemetery. He wanted to be buried in Hamburg; but, after some argument, that was not allowed. I don't recall going to the funeral. It may have been that children did not attend. His ashes were placed in a little box with a red ribbon around it. We didn't know what to do with them. I do remember being the one chosen to carefully carry them back to his home.

During that time, there was a great influx of Arabs in Hamburg. The women wore head cloths. They were very disliked in Germany. There would be signs saying, "Arabs stink" and things like that. To say that they smelled was an old way of expressing feelings against people of another background. All of a sudden Germany was populated with lots of people from other races and religions, which happened in America too; but Germany was and is a small country, so they made a bigger impact.

I remember thinking at the time that this negative racist attitude was in complete opposition to my family's liberal and totally humanistic point of view.

CHAPTER EIGHT
Curt Werner Bondy

**My Uncle
Curt Werner Bondy**

My Uncle, Curt Bondy[15], had an extraordinary story all his own.

When my Grandmother Marie Lauer Bondy died, she so was beloved that all of them, especially my Uncle

Curt, were very sad. My Father told my Mother that maybe if she went and slept with my Uncle it might ease his grief. So she offered this to him. His response surprised her. He replied, "No thank you, I am only attracted to men." Later, we all knew he was gay and he had a boyfriend for many, many years that I knew well and liked, but that was the first official notice to the family about his sexual preference.

In Germany at that time, homosexuality was much more accepted. However, among the first people the Nazis persecuted and killed were homosexuals.[16] I'm not sure why my Uncle was spared. He survived for many, many years and went on to contribute greatly to the world as a psychologist, a humanitarian and as an educator.

I was very close to Curt. For some reason, my Uncle considered himself the most ugly man in the world. This was hard to understand because the three brothers, my Father, Curt and his twin brother, Walter, looked very much alike and all were very handsome in my eyes. I often traveled with him and his boyfriend and we had many very funny adventures together.

My Uncle did some amazing things. He was well known as a very strong personality—very ethical, honest, forward thinking and, like the rest of my family, very highly educated. In 1933, along with Martin Buber[17], he co-founded the Jewish Center for Adult Education, which became very important as educational opportunities for Jews began to diminish. Among Curt's many achievements was the establishment of Gross-Breesen, a two-year agricultural program for Jewish teens.

Due to the Depression, many countries, including the U.S., placed strict restrictions on immigration. As we were to soon learn, visas were issued only for those with jobs waiting for them, relatives willing to support them, or for trained farmers. The goal of Gross-Breesen was to give young people skills which would allow them to emigrate from their country to places other than Israel, which some did not want to do.

Views of Gross-Breesen

In May 1936, along with the Central Association of German Jews, American William B. Thalhimer[18] purchased a 567-acre estate near the town of Breslau. William B. Thalhimer was a successful Virginia department store owner who sympathized with the plight of German Jews. Plans were already being made to create a similar school to give the students a place to emigrate to in the U.S. In 1938 he purchased Hyde Park Farm in Virginia and along with Curt, created an agricultural training center there modeled on Gross-Breesen. The students were made shareholders in the property, which made them eligible for non-quota emigration. Even so, it was a difficult and risky plan.

On November 9, 1938 came the terror of Kristallnacht. A bus arrived at Gross-Breesen and all of the boys over age eighteen were forced aboard and taken to Buchenwald concentration camp.

Ironically, I had just visited him at the school the day before this. My Uncle and the twelve boys were released after about one month thanks to the efforts of Mr. Thalhimer. After fifteen months of negotiations with the State Department, visas were finally secured for twenty-five Gross-Breesen students to come to the U.S.

From 1936-1940, 240 young people, including thirty girls, took part in the agricultural program at Gross-Breesen. Most who remained after 1940 were taken to concentration camps and the farm was turned into a German labor camp. Curt was able to escape this fate. In 1939, he immigrated to Holland and then with the rest of the family to the U.S.

Curt was the only one of our family to really embrace being Jewish. When he returned to Germany, he was one of the first Jewish scholars to be offered a position in academia. He became a Director and professor at the Psychologisches Institute of Hamburg until his retirement in 1959.

After the war, there were many black soldiers in Germany who had left behind multi-racial illegitimate children who were discriminated against and who had no care. My Uncle came back to Germany and created an organization for those children. That was typical of him and just one of many efforts he made on the part of others.

My Uncle put into practice the humanitarian concepts that my parents taught at Marienau. I really admired him for this.

The Marienau Experience

The Lake at Marienau

Life at Marienau was a true manifestation of my family's combined hopes, dreams and educational theories. They were given the opportunity to carry out their ideals, thanks in great measure to the backing of my Grandfather, Siegfried Bondy, who funded their schools.

Learning how to be yourself and developing your

own identity was more important than achievement at Marienau. Many of their precepts were easy for me to take for granted as a child, particularly the sense of being part of a community which was so integral to life at the school.

At one time, there were about 100 students at Marienau, which boarded students from fourth grade through high school. Few girls attended Marienau until they were officially admitted in 1928. The students truly owned the school. They participated in the decision making, including whom to admit. New students were voted to be a part of the community, after they had been at the school for a few weeks. It was a real, working democracy.

The basic ideas that life at Marienau was built upon included:

> Honesty
> Leadership
> Self-reliance
> Critical thinking
> Friendship
> Diversity
> Community
> Tolerance
> Mutual respect
> Equality of the sexes

The emphasis was not on the attraction of the sexes, or on love affairs (these happened), but on friendship and understanding and interest in each other as individual human beings, whether you were a child, an adult, a student, a teacher or part of the staff. People would take long walks together—that was one of our main activities—and just have thoughtful discussions.

64

View Across the Pond

Due to my Father's background as an art historian, art was naturally a major part of the experience at Marienau. Much of it expressed itself on the walls, where people would paint different pictures—especially the art teacher, Alfred Ehrhard, who did many impressionistic drawings. Art was everywhere, not only in the art teacher's room, but all over the campus.

Music was also a part of the day at Marienau in one way or another. We sang a lot of rounds. There was a lot of folk dancing—a different one every week—and I can still remember how to do them. The name of one of them was, in English: "I Put Glasses On My Eyes to See What The Books Are Like And That Is When I See Clearly That I Can't Live Without You." There was also very creative dance. For instance, there was one dance in the dark where everyone had gloves with lights on their fingers, so that all you saw were hands moving in the dark. I'm not sure how they created them, but it was something electric—very unusual, very creative. Dancing, painting, poetry, theater, sculpture—all of the arts were emphasized.

Something that always really impressed me about Marienau was the assemblies we would have. In these gatherings, even the youngest child had the freedom to speak up and they would be listened to. There wasn't a hierarchy. We would have discussions on a wide variety of subjects. Meditations on the meaning of life were a prominent part of the overall atmosphere. A great deal of time was spent thinking about our task in life. This occurred everywhere in the school. There was no special meeting room, although mostly students would gather in the foyer of the main building, sitting on the floor and even up the stairway. It was rather like a salon environment. My Father would speak or make announcements, usually each morning after breakfast. Almost every Sunday he gave what he called "Morning-Talks" on various topics such as courage and faith. Some of them were published in a small booklet in 1936.

In one, he expressed his feeling about the mystery of this existence:

We need not think about the sky full of stars which gives us a feeling of the boundlessness of the world, to feel, that this world includes something mighty and great in itself, which is not only unconceivable, but moving through its greatness and power.

Dr. Max Bondy
Morning-Talks

Following assembly, there would be gymnastics or a run of a mile or so, which I successfully avoided by having a stomachache much of the time—I hated running. Then there would be classes. They were very much traditional classes. Usually there were not more than maybe ten to fifteen students in each.

Language was considered very important. We had one hour of language six times a week, studying French for six years and English for eight. Everyone studied English at Marienau beginning in fourth grade. I had studied English from the time I was maybe four or five. Somehow my Mother had a premonition that we would need it and so we actually grew up bilingual. I also knew French quite well, though I've forgotten most it.

The American influence was great at that time and my Father was quite taken by it. He instituted "America Evening" where we would discuss American authors. We were big fans of Al Jolson's rendition of "Old Man River" and jazz music in general (although my Father somehow disapproved of jazz) and we would listen to these on those evenings.

The goal was to reach graduation, but it wasn't the curriculum that made it different. Schoolwork was kind of minor, although a wide range of reading was encouraged. The reading list included Kafka, Hesse and Freud, whose books were assigned as soon as they were published. Many of these books were later considered "un-German" and burned by the Nazis.

Physical labor and sports were also considered part of the fundamental ideas at Marienau. Students built their own sports playing field, digging up rocks and leveling the ground by hand with shovels and hoes. There was a first playing field up the hill called, "The Sand Hole." We used to spend hours climbing up and down the banks.

My parents felt that adolescence was a second opportunity to correct the mistakes that parents had made, and that happened when they got to Marienau. This was mostly due to my Mother, who was a very loving person. It was her idea that if you had the right relationship in your teen years to receive the love that your parents may have not given you, even if was from someone else, then you could change your life direction. As she remarked:

> *Adolescence is a time of no-man's-land. It is a very stormy time of loneliness and of seeking the goals and aims of life. The young people now have a hard time finding them and we try to help them. The problems are still the same as they have always been, only the solutions that the young people are trying to find are different. Some believe that the answers are in taking drugs, others in drinking or in a thoughtless and superficial life. Other generations have sought other remedies for their troubles. But we are not here to judge but to help them to find better ways of living a happy life.*

Dr. Gertrud Bondy
My Personal History[19]

My parents observed that parents, especially fathers, naturally wanted to raise their children in their own image. When parents became overcritical was when children withdrew from them. My Mother was able to reverse this by offering every child unconditional love. Many of the students who came to Marienau benefited from this. I think she saved a whole generation of young people. She was enormously beloved and admired by everyone. She was really the heart of the school.

Students Building the Sports Field
Marienau School / 1930s

Students Working
on the 'Chicken Church' Roof
Marienau School / 1960s

Although most of the students at Marienau were Caucasian, diversity was also celebrated.[20] There were twin sisters, who were black, who came from the south of Germany. It turned out that they were brilliant academically as well as talented. They sang beautifully. At the end of the year, when the best of the students were to be honored, they were getting all the awards. There was kind of an embarrassment among the student body and the parents that the ones who took home all the honors were the black girls. Everyone was amused, because it was against all the expectations or stereotypes or prejudice of the day. They were considered equal and somehow brought a very special flavor to the school. I remember laughing about it myself. I thought it was wonderful.

It was really what happened after school that made Marienau truly unique. The school day ended at two o'clock and after that there would be sports activities such as soccer, or field hockey and swimming in the summer, or ice hockey in the winter. Then, everyone would be totally on one's own. There was no tight supervision like there is in this country. You could go anywhere and do anything you wanted as long as you came back by dinnertime (probably hunger drove us back by that time, anyway.) I had a great deal of freedom, climbing trees and listening to people's conversations as they passed underneath and eating the cherries off the trees every fall until I got stomachaches.

My best friend at Marienau was Hannele, who later married another friend named Harald Baruschke. We were very close up until her death. My other very special friend was Adi Schlesinger.[21] We did everything together, especially getting into trouble, and he was a troublemaker most of the time. When we were maybe nine or ten and I had learned all about sex and where

70

My Best Friend Hannele
Marienau, early 1930s

babies came from, I told Adi about it and we decided we would teach the other children. We went around and told different children but I'm not sure they all believed us. They had been told different things, such as that the stork brings the babies. I have always thought that children should be told the truth once they show a curiosity, but parents really don't like it. They don't like their children to be told the truth, so children do their toilet talk and once they are told the truth it is okay. But it is really the parents who have the problem.

Adi and I were having private classes to learn Latin because we were going to go to university. We had this very boring teacher. All the rooms in the school were downstairs and you could just climb out of the

Adi Schlesinger as a Young Boy

window. One day, during a particularly boring class, an alarm clock started ringing just outside the window. The teacher, who was very big and heavy, climbed out and turned it off. He climbed back in and began teaching again. Then, another alarm clock went off. Adi had fixed five or six alarm clocks to go off at different times! He must have spent a fortune on alarm clocks but it was worth it because it disrupted the whole class.

When we were still children, Adi created a telephone line between my room and his. He did other things maybe not as funny, but dangerous. He was very knowledgeable about scientific things. He somehow put electricity into a doorknob and then put a wet cloth on it. You got quite a shock when you touched it. He kept us all amused.

Adi Schlesinger as a Teenager

There was a little girl who was somewhat mentally challenged. He told her that every night he went to America while she was asleep and then he would come back and tell her all the things that he saw there like the Indians and the Cowboys or what-not, so every day she was waiting for his stories. It was very touching.

Adi was always very ingenious. At one point he was the only Jewish student at Marienau other than myself, my siblings and one other boy—by that time there were less and less Jews in the school.

Both Adi and I felt very connected to nature. Marienau lay on the northeast edge of The Lüneburg Heath (Lüneburger Heide) just a mile or so from the town of Lüneburg[22]. The beauty of the landscape was so unusual; especially in the fall when the heather bloomed, with the shimmering birch trees in between, and the emergence of the Ginster, a plant with tiny yellow flowers that grew on the dry soil between the heather. There was a story by Andre Gide that I always identified with. I think he lays down in the grass or heather in a field and he smells the sweet smell of summer, then dies. I was very familiar with his works, which reminded me of the essence of Marienau. It was a very physical, as well as intellectual life. We were outside in nature as much as possible.

There was the pond right in front of the school. It wasn't very big, but there the Neetze River flowed into it. I must have been a teenager when my parents gave me a canoe. It was made of wood, as were the paddles. I never wore a life jacket—I don't think in those days you did that so much—also I don't think the lake was that deep. I can't remember if my siblings or the other children were jealous that I had a boat, but I was the only one allowed to have one. I would paddle up the river, enjoying steering the canoe and I got to be quite clever at it. I got so that I could paddle just on one side and I was very proud of that. I don't remember ever capsizing it or ever having anyone else in the boat with me. It was the only way that I felt I was special from the rest of the students at the school. I wish I still had it!

In winter we would ice skate on the lake, though I much preferred sledding and skiing. My Uncle Curt would do funny things at the lake. He had a Chevrolet, and he would drive the car out onto the frozen lake in the winter and put something into the steering wheel that would make the car go around and around by itself. He was always doing crazy things like that.

The Old Mill

You could swim in the lake, but I don't remember doing much of that. It was not really a swimming type of lake. There was a bridge across the river and I think at that time everybody smoked cigarettes, especially teen-agers. The cigarettes didn't have filters then. I must have smoked, but not very much—I didn't inhale—it was just kind of the thing to do, a matter of prestige rather than a desire to smoke.

If we wanted to smoke, we had to get permission and we had to do it across the bridge behind the old mill where electricity was made by a large water wheel. We only had electricity half the time and it originally came from that old mill. The mill was also the place you went to be alone with your boyfriend.

Most of all, I loved to ride my bicycle around Marienau. I could go "no-handed." My bicycle had a bell, a light and a basket on the front, with a flat seat in the back so someone could ride with you. It might have been a Christmas or a birthday present.

My bicycle was a woman's bicycle. Like those today, it didn't have a bar in the middle. You got onto it from the side. In those days girls didn't wear pants, so I rode in a long skirt and cotton knee socks, pedaling it from one side, which was not an easy thing to do.

I rode all over Marienau and to the little towns nearby. What you had to learn to do was ride on a small path on the side of the road because you couldn't really go in the middle of the road—there was no space for bicycles. We would often ride to Lüneburg. It would take twenty minutes or so. We all rode bicycles, even my Father. My Mother, on the other hand, would never have done anything so ordinary. She would have considered it unladylike.

I remember also that there was one very vicious boy at the school. One day he put a string across the road with the intention that people would go fast on their bicycles and it would hit their throat. Someone discovered this and my Father became incensed about it as someone might have been killed or really hurt that way.

You'd also become very dirty traveling on the dusty roads. In those days you had to wait until there were three or four spots on things before you cleaned them because everything was hand washed. To iron clothes we used what we called a "mangle" which consisted of a metal roller that you heated up on the stove or later, on an electric base. I was terrible at ironing, so fortunately we had someone do our laundry for us.

My parents orchestrated everything that went on at the school. Food was always a major undertaking. It wasn't easy to feed over 100 people, particularly during the Depression.[23] There were five meals served during the day. The first breakfast was served at seven o'clock in the morning, usually something light like an egg and a piece of toast, followed by second breakfast a few hours later, which consisted of some bread and butter and cold cuts. Then came a big lunch at one o'clock (which, until the Depression, always had a soup course). This was a formal affair where everyone had to sit down and be served. Coffee time came around five o'clock with sweets and then dinner. Sometimes we were served a midnight snack.

My Father had a ritual at lunch where everyone had to lift their fork up and to the left and right and then down into their food in unison before everyone began eating. It was very amusing. We all loved that ritual. There was a blind boy at Marienau who managed quite well. He sat next to another child and kept getting his food off the plate of the other child, and no one stopped him. There was a genuine spirit of generosity where there was a lot of respect for each human being. There was much politeness at the table, but like all normal children, there was always mischief. We often kicked each other under the table or flung peas at each other when no one was looking.

At Marienau, most of the meals were served at the dining room tables. The food was brought up on an elevator from the kitchen in the basement. There were no assigned seats—you just sat where you wanted. There was a staff that took care of the cooking and cleaning; but when money was tight, students did a lot of the cleaning and other chores in the kitchen.

The Chicken Church

One thing I remember vividly was something we had called "potato vacation." We would go and pick our own potatoes so we would have some food. Since the school also owned a little land right around it, we grew potatoes and other vegetables and raised chickens, which helped sustain the students at the school. There was a little house that had a clock on its tower called "The Chicken Church" (Die Hühnerkirche). The chickens were raised in and around that house. Why it had a clock, I don't know. It must have been one of the original outbuildings.

The German people were suffering greatly from hunger and other deprivations at the time. We were great bread eaters and we were used to sandwiches that were covered with butter and marmalade. During that time, due to shortages and in the interest of frugality, we would get only two slices at a time—one covered with butter, the other with marmalade. I remember that we would take the butter-sided bread and the marmalade-sided bread and rub them together so that they would have a little of each on them.

**Outdoor Class at Marienau
(After a Night of Dancing)**

You were expected to be at meals on time, but I don't remember any repercussions if you were late. There might be "consequences," which were slightly different. For example, if you threw sand in the eyes of other children at the sandbox, you were removed from the sandbox. Or, if you went on a school trip and misbehaved, you might be sent home. There were rules like 'no running in the halls' and logical consequences for those. Other than that, there were no punishments whatsoever at Marienau. As a result of that, and of having a great deal more freedom, students misbehaved a lot less. It truly was an island unto itself.

Because I was the daughter of the Directors, I was always a little bit of an exception at Marienau; consequently, I really wasn't treated like everyone else. The children often shied from me and wouldn't include me in any mischief because they thought I would tell on them. On occasion they would allow me to participate in some misdeed, usually a minor one.

To illustrate this, everything concerning food had to be carefully planned. So that they would last longer, all the baskets of apples and potatoes and other perishables were kept cool in the basement. A kind of funny episode developed from this. The apples were stored separately in the cellar of a barn connected with the school. There was a kind of walkway around the upper part of the barn. Slowly, the apples began to dwindle, without anyone really knowing why.

Finally, someone in my family realized that some of the students had developed a method of putting a knife at the end of a long string and spearing the apples that way. At first, the other students didn't think they would let me do it, mostly because I was the daughter of the Directors. I had to beg them. Finally, they let me. It wasn't easy to "fish" for the apples that way, but it was great fun. When my Father found out about how the apples disappeared, he lined everyone up who was guilty. He was quite upset. He was, of course, very surprised to see me in the line. He said to me, "Et tu?" I don't think we were punished. In fact, I think it kind of secretly amused him, because it was such an inventive trick.

In addition to all the music and art at Marienau, we put on a lot of plays. I acted in "A Midsummer's Night Dream" and a musical, "We're Building a New Town Just for Children," which was a very pretty operetta. The chairs had to be moved from the dining room to the stage for performances. We made a line, handing chairs from one to the other in a link to do this, instead of carrying each chair, which was pretty clever.

We also had a lot of festivals. Parents were invited. There were plays and music and sports activities and so on, with many reasons for celebrations. One of them was on my Father's birthday where people lined up and formed the word, 'Max.'

Students Spell Out the Word 'Max'

In February of that year, we heard about the burning of the German Parliament building (Reichstag). Most people believed that the Nazis did this themselves to discredit the Communist Party. After that, the Nazis became the majority party, allowing Hitler to consolidate his power.

Then, one day, in 1933, when I was about to turn sixteen, I looked out my window and saw an orange ocean of people marching towards the school. The S.A. (Sturm Abteilung or storm troopers, also known as "Brown Shirts") were the Nazi paramilitary. They were well known for their brutal policing of anyone opposed to the Nazis. I knew what and who they were and they were a fearsome sight.

For some reason, they had decided to participate in our school festival and there was nothing we could do. My Mother suddenly had to provide food for 200 more people. Even though it had been a fun and festive day, once again it was like there was a dark, ominous cloud in front of the sun.

CHAPTER TEN
Jewishness

Annemarie, Age 15

It was a frightening time. There was so much we didn't understand. Without a doubt, it was a most perilous time to be a Jew.

My Grandfather was very liberal and freethinking and many of his friends were artists and intellectuals, but they couldn't escape the stereotypes associated with being Jewish. My Grandfather didn't particularly want to be a Jew. He thought it was better for his business to be thought of more as German rather than Jewish. In fact, he changed his name from Salomon Bondy to Siegfried Bondy in order to seem more Aryan. Much of the anti-Semitism of the time grew out of the belief that the Jews had gotten very rich in Germany and owned all the department stores.

My Father, like my Grandfather, never wanted to be identified as a Jew. He really thought of himself as Bohemian rather than Jewish because his ancestors had come from Spain to Czechoslovakia and intermarried so frequently with the villagers there. Somehow he tried to construe a story that he was really the son of Frau Winsemann, my Grandfather's housekeeper. This was pretty far-fetched. Everyone made a bit of fun of this, but he thought it would make him a Gentile. Later he fell in love with Frau Winsemann's daughter, Grete (Margaret) Duschenes, who was married to a good friend of ours. I played with her four sons later on. I'm sure this was after he was married to my Mother because I remember him sending a postcard with a love letter to her, with my picture on the other side.

Perhaps because he was so open-minded, my Uncle Curt was the only one who didn't seem conflicted by this. He accepted who he was. But our family as a whole never really thought of ourselves or identified with being Jewish. Even then there was the perception that the Jews had all the money and much as they tried they really couldn't erase that stereotype. They were admired, but also looked down upon. Nevertheless, most of our friends were Jewish and we grew up happily in the German culture.

My parents' humanist philosophy grew out of the German Youth Movement, which began in Berlin in 1896. Originally called "Wandervogel" (wanderbirds) or later, "Jugendbewegung" (youth movement), German Jugendbewegung was based on very high ideals. It encouraged members "To run our lives according to our decisions, responsible to ourselves and in absolute truth."[24]

The movement arose at a time when there was a very dishonest way of domestic living. People were married, but most men had mistresses or went to prostitutes. They believed in total freedom for themselves, but not for women. This way of living life was totally accepted at the time. In fact, the wives almost welcomed it, because they didn't have to exert themselves. It was a very conservative time.

The German Youth Movement, which was composed of many different groups from right wing to left wing, rebelled against this double standard. They believed in being honest and in the romanticism of going back to nature and being as natural and adventurous as possible. They did a lot of folk dancing, which was so much fun. The girls dressed in long flowing skirts and didn't wear makeup. This seemed almost sloppy in comparison to the strait-laced fashions then. The boys wore simple clothing, also against the fashion of the time, when men wore suits and hats so that they could tip their hat to their neighbors when they passed by. The Youth Movement opposed the dishonest standards of the day. They were rather like the hippies in the 1960s in the U.S. in that way.

As a young man, my Father was very involved in The Youth Movement as a leader. His four younger brothers at the time were also very involved. On the other hand, my Mother, who was always very elegant, didn't want to be a part of it. She stuck to her own sense of high fashion, but she didn't fight the ideas of the movement. She agreed with the philosophy.

Later, the Hitler Youth, created in the 1920s, personified German discipline. There were separate organizations for boys and girls. The boys focused on militaristic athletics such as marching, grenade throwing, map reading and pistol shooting. The girls practiced running, marching and swimming, as well as domestic activities preparing them for motherhood. It mushroomed rapidly. By 1936, the Hitler Youth had four million members. By 1938, it had grown to eight million children, all singing and marching to Hitler's anthems.

It may have been in the beginning of the Nazi period when my Father was told to withdraw from The Youth Movement because he was a Jew. He was a very devoted German. He loved Germany intensely. He felt like he really knew what being German was all about. The fact that they asked him to leave the group he belonged to because of his heritage absolutely devastated him.

There was a man at that time who invented a way of measuring a person's head structure and determining whether they were Jewish. My Father had his head measured, but I don't remember whether they determined if he was Jewish by this method or not. They tried to put this on a scientific basis, inventing a whole pseudo-science, but we all scoffed at it.

When I was about eleven years old, I was on a school trip in Gdansk. We were walking through the streets and some children were throwing stones at us and making anti-Semitic remarks. I was both terrified and mystified. I said to this other boy—"I don't understand. There are no Jews here." The boy said, "Yes there are. You and me." It sounds strange, but that was when I first really understood that I was Jewish.

You must understand that many people during that time grew up thinking of themselves simply as

Germans, not Jews. My Father was a very convinced Christian and believed strongly in Christian ideals.

**Class Trip to Gdansk, Denmark
(Annemarie with Headscarf)**

At Christmas, we would put all the presents on tables around the room. Then the doors would be flung open and we would all come rushing in. Each child had his or her presents in the same location each year. It was the custom then to have a wreath, a Christmas tree and a wreath around the chandelier. We celebrated the Advent days and my Father would read, "The Night Before Christmas" to the children. We had real candles on the Christmas tree and on Christmas itself we would take them and put them on an outdoor tree and stand around and sing carols like, "Silent Night" and "O Tannenbaum." We usually had a goose at Christmas or a turkey, but no stuffing. That, I learned later, was an American tradition.

We always had a big party at Marienau because some of the children didn't go home at Christmas. Many of the rooms would be empty, of course, and this is where all my relatives would stay, sometimes as many as thirty people. Sometimes we had Christmas dinner at my Grandfather's house and then if Hanukkah happened to be close to Christmas that year, we would all go next door to my Aunt Nelly's house. She was the only one who celebrated Hanukkah. My Father detested wearing a yarmulke. He would always make fun of it. Once, he donned one of my Aunt Nelly's hats instead, then surreptitiously made faces at me at the dinner table while I tried very hard not to laugh.

Even before the Nazis, there was always that conflict in our family regarding our Jewishness. It was something that simmered in the background, resulting in my Father and all of my Uncles serving in the German Army as volunteers in WWI, in part in order to hide their Jewishness, but mostly to express their dedication to their country. However, they never were successful in the Army. They were never promoted or allowed to rise above a certain rank. My Father's brother, Walter, was killed by friendly fire while serving at the front.

In 1924, when I was six, we all became baptized as Lutherans at the same time, including all of my cousins. My brother Heinz was a newborn baby then. There were a number of families we knew who also participated. My Mother, particularly, thought it might save us from being discriminated against, although I wasn't aware of that then. I only remember as there having been a strange kind of dishonesty in the air that day.

Despite being confirmed as Lutherans, it was not long before we were identified as being Jewish when, in

1933, the Nazis began infiltrating the school. Because of this, my brother was not allowed to participate in the Hitler Youth and my sister and I were excluded from the girls division, the BDM (Bund Deutche Madchen.)

This affected Heinz deeply. He was twelve years old at the time. He was blonde and blue-eyed and looked the part of the perfect Aryan. When he was rejected by the Hitler Youth, he felt very isolated because every other child was obligated to participate in it and they were having fun, going on camping and hiking trips and playing games. He loved sports, especially soccer, and he just couldn't understand why he was excluded.

My Brother Heinz's Little Car

Fortunately, someone (probably my Grandfather) had a small car built for him that ran on gasoline and that he could actually drive around the campus. There was a very famous race driver then and he pretended to be that person. This was a great source of delight for him. I've often wondered what became of that little car.

My sister lived in England then where she was going to boarding school. I don't recall feeling at all excluded. I lived in my own dream world most of the time and despite the Nazi presence, I felt very protected by my parents and the community at Marienau. It did, however, enter my personal life later, in a way that I have never forgotten.

**Marienau Students
with Teacher Karl Storch**

George Roeper, who was a student at Marienau, was to become the love of my life, but at that time there was another man in love with me. Karl Storch was a teacher and I was in love with him, too, although I was unofficially betrothed to George. George was away at University then and would come home to visit only on holidays. Karl and I would walk in the heather and read the works of Rainer Maria Rilke. At Marienau, lovers would always meet outdoors. I was only fifteen and he was very careful with me. Once he came very close to seducing me, but then decided against it.

Someone spied on us and he was warned about having a forbidden relationship with a Jewish girl, which had become illegal under the "race-shame" laws.[25] He left the next day and enlisted in the German army before he could be arrested. He wrote me several letters while at the front. In one, he told me that he imagined that while he was in the trenches, he would see a butterfly. It would remind him of me and that he would forget being in a foxhole and stand up and be shot. Later his fantasy became true—he stood up while in a foxhole and he was killed.

I always carried a terrible sense of guilt that I could cause someone harm, whether directly or indirectly. My parents' philosophies were in direct opposition to the corruption of the times. It was quite a revolution. Theirs was a very progressive point of view, much like that of John Dewey in the United States, but went much further than that. They also believed in free love. Any honest relationship was acceptable. Men and women were on equal terms. It was perhaps the very beginning of the women's movement, which brought German women beyond the three K's which defined them: Kinder (children), Kirche (church) and Kuche (kitchen). Even so, when I grew up, I believed somehow that the wife is more dominated by the husband. That is how pervasive that notion continued to be.

My parents also felt that it was important to make

a contribution to the world and to try and make it a better place, as well as to create community. There was no room for discrimination by race or sex or religion in their worldview. They emphasized being a part of the mystery that surrounds us.

Life at Marienau fostered a kind of creative and personal freedom that doesn't exist in many places. We lived in great freedom to follow our own star, but we also felt very secure. It was so carefree. I could go wherever I wanted to go or do what I wanted to do without asking permission. I never thought about whether people were black or white or Christian or Jewish. I didn't know anything else. Until, that is, the Nazis came and my whole world, as I knew it, began to unravel.

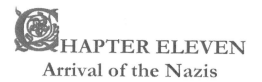

CHAPTER ELEVEN
Arrival of the Nazis

Marienau
Under the Nazis

It was after that summer festival in 1933 that the Nazi influence began to be felt at the school. By 1935 they had completely taken over the campus. It happened slowly at first, starting with the teachers. There were many that were not Nazis, but most of them were cowards and it became a matter of great danger. For instance, every morning, we were forced to start the day by saying 'Heil Hitler,' followed then by our usual Bach concerto. Then, before long, we were forced to say it before every class started. Soon the Nazi flag was being flown over the school.

A curriculum was then imposed that was geared

towards Nazi ideas. There was the regular old-fashioned curriculum being taught in all the German schools, but this was somehow besides that. No one took it very seriously. It was transmitted by a lot of singing and stomping around. There was one song I will never forget: the title of it was: "When Jewish Blood Springs From the Knife, We Will be Happy."

We often devised ways of defending ourselves from the negativity enveloping us. We had something called "The Pencil War." I had a pencil that had four colors and that was unusual at that time. Everybody wanted that pencil and so some boys decided to steal it and then some girls were ready to steal it back. So then we got into a whole war. Boys were hiding in my closet to see if they could find my pencil. This game would interrupt the classrooms. We would hide the pencil while the teacher was teaching and it became a very big fun thing. It was something my parents would never have allowed to happen if they'd known about it, since the Nazis were there. Then one day it was decided that The Pencil War was over and we had a big party and ice cream and cake.

There were many strange things happening at that time. The Hitler Youth had collected some money and it disappeared. It was revealed that the money had chemicals on it that could determine who had touched it. The students were locked in a room to see if any of their hands showed that they had touched the money. My Mother suspected that the person who took it was the one who collected it. It turned out that she was right—it was a boy who was the leader of the Hitler Youth at the school. His parents were so ashamed of him that they sent him to school in Africa and rejected their son completely.

For a time, around 1936, the boys at Marienau,

including George Roeper, were encouraged to become part of the Nazi S.A. as a strategy to protect them if they were confronted by the Nazis outside of the school. This only lasted for six months, when it was required for them to join a different group and they managed to avoid registering for it.

I quickly learned that you never could tell what people would do. Our art teacher, Alfred Ehrhard, was married to a Jewish woman and during this period he divorced her, saying there was no choice. That was common in those days, but I found it to be very shocking.

The ideals of Marienau were in total opposition to those of Hitler. Germans, in general, were steeped in a tradition of masculine dominance and leadership at that time. In my parents' school, a very free and democratic environment existed. We became an island in a sea of strict paternal dominance that traditionally pervaded the educational system as well as the family.

Obedience was the greatest virtue in the Germany in which I grew up. Children in German families were truly to be seen but not heard. I remember a German teacher saying proudly, "If I tell my students to jump out of a fourth story window, which would certainly lead to their death, I know that they would obey immediately." I later felt that this was the basis for the Nazi's ability to grow. Despite our ideals, my family was very much rooted in the German tradition but our Jewish background was mostly forgotten. From my personal experience, the rise of the Nazis was rather not anticipated—but it should have been.

One of the things that contributed to the Nazis popularity was the state of the economy then. After WWI Germany was required to pay a large amount of reparation money and financially the country deteriorated more and more. It was also a time of great inflation, which devalued any existing money. I don't remember actually being hungry, but I still remember it as a very bad and frightening time. Hitler implemented things like "one-pot suppers" and "winter care" which subtly persuaded people that he was their savior.

During that time, my Grandfather gave both my sister and I 200,000 marks. This was probably equivalent to $500,000 back then, which was still quite a bit of money. It was meant to be our dowry for when we got married. Even at that time the idea of a dowry offended me because I didn't think that anyone needed to find a man or to buy me—I thought I was valuable enough by myself. In any event, due to hyperinflation, the value of German money dwindled so quickly and to such an extent that my Mother decided to use what was left to buy a pair of stockings for each of us.

As time went on, the Nazis would come and inspect the school on a regular basis. We were able to keep the school open due to my Mother's skill as a psychoanalyst. There was a very high-ranking Nazi official who worked in the Ministry of Education, who had a teenage girl named Ursula Kerrl, who was very difficult.

Hermann Goering's wife was a friend of the Kerrl's and they were told that the only person who could help the child was my Mother, so the girl was sent to Marienau. This protected us for four years, but increasingly we were living under their rules and regulations. At one point, I recall that Goerring himself made a personal visit to the school.

One of our students was a great believer in the Nazis. Although he was dark haired himself, he thought that Hitler's ideas of a nation of blonde and blue-eyed people was a wonderful one. The students disliked him and were always playing tricks on him. One night they gave him a sleeping pill and put peroxide on his head and he woke up blonde, because that is what he always wanted to be. When he woke up, I think he was very surprised and then angry, but the students had great fun doing it.

It was a strange period where people either proved their courage—or not. You had a pretty good idea of who was supporting you, but you never really knew who was your friend or your enemy. More and more it became a matter of not knowing who could be trusted. There were certain people that you knew you could talk to who understood how we hated the whole thing. There were others you could not say anything like that to. It was simply the antithesis of what my parents believed in. The only way of surviving was by having a sense of humor. Fortunately, my Father really loved to laugh and he encouraged this.

There came a point when the Nazis would not allow Jews to educate Aryan children and my parents were informed that they had to give up the school. It was then sold to a young teacher named Dr. Bernhard Knoop and the school continued on under his ownership, although with a much more conservative curriculum. My Father was despondent and it was so difficult to see my parents, so strong and independent and free-thinking, be so constrained and so completely powerless under the Nazis.

It literally broke my heart.

CHAPTER TWELVE
George Roeper

George Roeper as Young Man

    I was five years old when one day a thirteen-year-old boy appeared at my parents' school at Gandersheim. He was the most handsome boy that I had ever seen. This was not just my opinion. Every photograph from those early days will bear that out.

My first experience with him was a strange one. He must have been talking to me, and was pointing toward me with his finger telling me something. His finger got caught in my mouth and I think I bit it. I was really just a little girl.

My First Meeting
With George Roeper

George had soft brown eyes and brown hair. We called him "Geoli" or "Little George." He arrived at our school all by himself. He didn't want his Mother to bring him because he wanted to be seen as an independent person. He was sent to our boarding school at the advice of his public school teacher who realized that George's Father was truly a cruel man whose two sons disliked him to such an extent that they looked forward to when their Father left for work each morning.

He felt equally at home at Gandersheim and, later, at Marienau. Hans Wolf Wachsmann, his best friend, was also extremely handsome. At that time, precocious child that I was, I was deeply in love with Hans Wolf—which I then later transferred to George. One day when I happened to be in the kitchen, Hans Wolf walked by. There was a huge pot filled with cold water and potatoes soaking by the stove and I was so taken with him that I fell backwards into the water. Everyone laughed, but I was mortified. That water was freezing!

Hans Wolf Wachsmann

I don't exactly remember when George's and my relationship became so close but I know I was no more than eleven when I had a car accident and a severe concussion. I was on a school trip when it happened. In those days there were so few cars. Somehow I was on the other side of the street from the rest of the group. I saw an airplane (still a rare occurrence then) and when I ran back to tell the others, a car hit me. I fell and bruised my head and went unconscious.

A teacher named Marta Phillip was in charge of the trip. She took me to a hospital and I woke up and said, "Is this heaven?" because I thought I was dead. This surprised me, because I didn't believe in heaven. Then, it was very difficult, because I was away from home and my parents. The trip leader couldn't stay with me so somehow my Father came to pick me up at the hospital. He had a car where you could put the seat all the way back, so they laid me down in there and took me home to the school. There was a special room at the school just for sick people.

I had to stay in bed for three months after that because of the concussion and I wasn't allowed to move. It was during that time that George and I became so close. He visited me every day at my bedside. We were both very enamored of Van Gogh. The letters between Vincent and his brother were quite beautiful and had just been published and we read them together and discussed them. We talked a lot and philosophized, wondering if there was a God or not—all the things we still don't know much about.

I think we were in love already at that time, which I remember enraged some of the other girls. One of them, Gabriella Derenberg, came from the Warburg[26] family, who very wealthy Jews, but she was most unattractive. Adi, one of my best friends and playmates, always imitated the strange way she walked—like she was rowing a boat. She came to me and said, "It's not fair. You are only ten years old and I am fifteen and

George never looks at me and only you." She was quite angry with me about it. But it was true.

George began to play a very important role in the school at that time. For many years he was the leader of the student government and kept meticulous notes on all the meetings and discussions. I think those notes may be somewhere in the archives at Marienau.

George and I were intertwined like some trees that grow into each other and around each other. We had a great deal in common. I was very mature for my age and very interested in art and nature and literature. It was probably a strange picture when people would see this eighteen-year-old boy and the ten-year-old girl go into the woods together, always carrying a book.

If such a relationship developed today, people would have been concerned about it, thinking there might be something wrong with it; that it was not proper. Our family's attitude and society's attitude in general towards relationships and sex after WWI were quite different. (It was also different in America than in Germany.) My Mother; however, saw nothing wrong with the relationship and was very supportive of it. One day she gave us permission to go on a trip for several days. We slept in the same bed together, although he didn't touch me. But that night—I was eleven by that time—I told him I felt this strange trickle between my legs and it turned out to be my first menstruation. Luckily, I was totally informed about everything and was able to handle it immediately.

Ever since then, it was officially known that George and I belonged together. We had very definite plans for our future in Germany at that time. Like my parents, we were going to start a boarding school and educate children so they would be helpful and useful citizens in this world. But then, the Nazis took over and my family began to think about leaving the country. It was George who insisted that we should leave for America. My Father did not want to go, but George understood that it was a matter of life and death. He was the one who actually facilitated our move to America.

George also came from a wealthy family. I remember someone saying that the family made their money from love, which was true. There was an area in the city called Reperbehn where the prostitutes hung out. George's family owned part of that property. All of that, however, was before my time.

Georg Paul Röper
Georg Alexander Hermann Röper
Johann "Hanns" Ludwig
Georg Röper

George was born Georg Alexander Hermann Röper in Hamburg, Germany on September 7, 1910 to George Paul Röper[27] and Anna Meyer. Anna was a very

104

warm, affectionate kind person. His Father was an engineer and also had an import and export business, bringing coffees and teas to Germany, and tools and steel to Japan, which was taken over from his own Father. By all accounts he was a very severe, tyrannical man to his family. The children received only one kiss a year, on Christmas.

Anna Meyer Röper

George spent the first four years of his life in Kyoto, Japan, where his Father had a company that sold steel for the construction of the Trans-Siberian Railway. When George returned, he spoke no German—only Japanese, although later he lost all his fluency. His older brother, Johann "Hanns" Ludwig Georg[28] was born in Japan in 1905.

His Father always preferred George to Hanns, but one day while walking with his sons along the river in Hamburg, he said, "I don't know why I don't toss you both into the river." Their Mother stayed married because of the children, but seriously considered divorce.

George went to public school and became very close to a teacher who soon realized how abusive George's Father was to his sons, especially Hanns.

**George Roeper
as an Infant in Japan**

The teacher knew Max through a Youth Movement group they both belonged to, and so he went to George's parents to recommend sending George to the school at Gandersheim.

George was most eager to go away to school. He hid outside the door and eavesdropped on the discussion. Finally, his Father agreed—it would be socially prestigious for his son to attend boarding school. His brother Hanns, who was not so academically inclined, never went to Gandersheim or Marienau, although he did work for a time as my Father's secretary. He later became a journalist.

Shortly before his graduation from Marienau, George's Father died and his Mother then moved to Merano, Italy in 1932. George's Father had moved much of their money there to evade taxes and she lived there until she died of a stroke in 1935 at the age of fifty-five. George was in his fourth year at university. My parents really became substitute parents for George from then on.

After graduation, George attended the University of Munich and later received a master's degree from the University of Berlin. His father wished him to study finance and go into business. While working on his Ph.D. in economics, his dissertation was on the role of government banks in student loans. He began his doctoral degree in at Greifswald, but never received it because he became involved in helping us immigrate to the U.S.[29]

Both my parents were very fond of George. He became part of the family almost immediately and as he became more and more involved in the leadership at the school, he became a very well respected member of the community at Marienau.

One summer, while my family was traveling in Switzerland looking for a new site for a school, George and I decided to elope while my parents took a trip to Italy. We made an elaborate plan to elude the friends of my parents we were staying with. When my parents discovered this, they were very angry, mostly with George, because they felt I was too young. So we were not married at that time, only engaged.

One morning a uniformed Nazi S.S. man

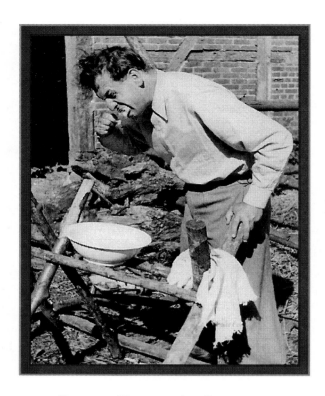

George Roeper in Germany

suddenly appeared in George's apartment. This shocked George terribly. Everybody knew what they did as part of Hitler's protection force. Fortunately, the man had been a former student of my parents and he let George, who was not Jewish, know he was now on a list of those to be shot on sight for being friendly with Jews. At that moment, George realized that he had to flee the country. He had put aside a little money with which he bought an equal amount of gold. Our family didn't have much to add to this. Most of our money was tied up in the school property.

He made a somewhat brilliant plan. He melted down the gold and made them into bricks and blackened them, then somehow stuck them under his car. He knew he was in the so-called S.S. "black book," so he dressed himself up in mountain climbing gear and drove to the smallest checkpoint. There was only one man at the Swiss border. George pointed to the mountain that was close by and at the moment the man looked up, he slipped through the crossing. That is really how he got out of Germany. He would later join us in Switzerland.

George Roeper, Annemarie, Gertrud, Max, Heinz, Ulla, Curt Bondy

George's brother Hanns and his wife Edith Sowade Roper[30] played an important part in family history at this time. During Kristallnacht[31] or "The Night of Broken Glass" they were able to save fifteen Jewish friends, including my cousin Peter, by sheltering them in their apartment. This was a very courageous act, as they could have been sent to a concentration camp or killed. Hanns didn't feel that this was courageous. He felt that it was the right thing to do—and that there really was no choice involved.

As Hanns had been born in Japan, this allowed Edith and himself to be granted visas to the U.S. under the small Japanese quota. Edith, who had been a journalist and then a court reporter, was able to smuggle her notes documenting the abuses of the Nazi legal system out of Germany to Switzerland and then to the U.S.

While en route, Hanns was intercepted and arrested in Paris and taken to a concentration camp, but freed in November 1939. The two then arrived in the U.S. on January 8, 1940, where Edith wrote her exposé <u>Skeleton of Justice</u>, published by E.P. Dutton in 1941.

Hanns and Edith Roper

It was George who took care of many of the loose ends in Germany for us. He really became the hero of my family. Due to George's foresight our family began, along with many other Jewish families, the very stressful and complicated process of emigration.

CHAPTER THIRTEEN
Graduation and Emigration

Last Day at Marienau

My Father and I never really spent much time alone together except for what we shared at the end of our time at Marienau. In 1937, I was just getting ready to graduate from high school, so it was agreed that we would stay until then.

It was a strange graduation because it was under

the Nazis. In fact, two classes graduated that year, as more people were needed for the war effort. One of the questions I had to answer during my oral examination was the difference between culture and civilization. The answer they expected was: the world is a civilized world, but the Germans have culture. (With that they meant the Nazis, of course.) I was asked that question and I knew that this was the answer I was supposed to give, but I couldn't do it. They passed me anyway. It was pretty conceited and transparent on their part and just another example of the mental control they tried to exact upon us.

My Father thought at first that the Hitler's dominance was a passing phase. But when it became clear what the Nazis had in mind, my Father fell into a deep depression and he began to suffer from a terrible blood illness, polycythemia; which, ironically, is a disease that affects mostly Jewish people. It was probably one of the most tragic experiences of my life to watch him when the Nazis were already there and when he had to hand over Marienau to Dr. Bernhard Knoop[32], the man appointed to officially own the school.

Marienau was sold to Dr. Knoop for 180,000 marks (worth about $448,200 then.) A penalty of 58,000 marks was imposed by the Nazis for a forced repayment of mortgages. Another 50,000 marks were placed in a "blocked account" of the Dresdner Bank, then owned by the Third Reich. This was all part of the process of "linearization," during which Jews were forced to sell their property and possessions to Aryans. Needless to say, the money my Father received for the land and the school was a pittance and only a fraction of its true worth. They basically ended up with nothing.

My Mother had already had taken my brother and sister to Switzerland, so just my Father and I were left at

Marienau with the remaining students.

I was hoping that my Father would share some of his pain with me and that it would bring the two of us closer, but he wasn't interested in being close to me. I would watch him more or less from a distance and felt so desperately that I wanted to help him, but that he didn't want my help.

At the same time, of course, I had my own pain. It was a bitter disappointment that Germany didn't want me. I felt that my heart was broken into a million pieces —that is really the only way to describe it. The pain was so great that I couldn't bear it and I don't know if my Father could either. It was then that I put away all the feelings that I had.

I remember so clearly our last moment at Marienau. We got in the car and my Father made "the honor round," circling several times around the square in front of the school, as he always did when we were leaving on a long journey. On the last trip around the square, it felt like I was dying. I knew I couldn't bear the pain, that I would have to turn off my feelings or I wouldn't survive it. And then, we started out. It was too difficult to look back.

The day after graduation, my Father and I fled to Switzerland. My Mother had already begun another school there in Gland near Lake Geneva. The school, called "Les Rayons," was being was run by another of my parents' students, Harald Baruschke. Harald also wanted to marry me, but I had already decided that it was George who would accompany me to America.

By 1938, Les Rayons sheltered more than fifty-five students between the ages of six and fifteen. Eventually children from Czechoslovakia, Austria, England and the Netherlands joined the other German refugee students[33] at the school as Hitler began to threaten those countries. Both George and I taught there along with thirteen other teachers.

Courses were offered in mathematics, science, history, music and French, German and English languages. There was also an emphasis on handicrafts such as cookery, needlework, knitting, carpentry, wood-carving, leatherwork, mechanics and photography. As at Marienau, physical education was considered very important. Each day there were lessons in gymnastics, cross-country running, football, basketball, tennis or, in winter, snow skiing. In summer, the students enjoyed swimming, rowing and motor boating on Lake Geneva—it was quite beautiful there—as well as mountain excursions into the Savoy and Valais Alps.

Les Rayons continued the ideal of community education that my parents had begun at Marienau, which required the teachers and even the youngest of the students to lend their voice to the running of the school. Their humanistic philosophy took on an even greater sense of urgency:

> *In many Sunday morning talks, and in private conversations, our school aim has been referred to, which is, to take care that there must be men and women whose highest aim is to be self-responsible, chivalrous and truthful. It has become more and more evident to us how important such an aim is at the present time, when the tendency is becoming stronger and stronger to replace self-responsibility by mass-suggestion, truthfulness by opportuneness, and chivalry by utilizing the force of the stronger against the weaker, or even the defenceless, as a moral principle. We have*

Dr. Max Bondy
and Dr. Gertrud Bondy
Report of the Ecole, Les Rayons,
Gland, December, 1938

My Father was despondent at that point. He didn't really participate. He was a changed person and my Mother seemed to do everything. I worked at the school until it was time to continue my education.

When I was eighteen, I had just enrolled in the University of Vienna where I was studying medicine in order to later become a psychoanalyst. I remember taking chemistry and anatomy and working on corpses, including examining a foot and having to memorize all of the different muscles. I got used to this fairly easily. I was planning to study child psychoanalysis, which was not a course being offered, but something that Anna Freud was in the process of creating. Anna Freud was an extremely bright person; very logical, and later her book, Normalcy and Pathology in Childhood: Assessment of Development became the basis of my work with children. I also met Bruno Bettleheim at that time, but I had an instant dislike for him. I felt that he had a very aggressive personality.

I only studied there for about six months before I became very sick with mononucleosis. My Godmother, Pauline, took care of me and I lived with her for some time. She lived at Begrstrausse 9, opposite Bergstrausse 19 where Freud lived. My Mother arranged a meeting with them, which was a rare privilege.

In order to study with Anna and Sigmund Freud, you had to be twenty-one to be more mature. That day

115

is very vivid in my mind. I spent two hours talking with
Freud and his daughter, Anna, in his typically Austrian
office filled with all sorts of art and things he collected.
It was very cozy and cluttered. There were mementos
and pictures everywhere, heavy carpets and drapes, and
a bedspread on the sofa where he rested. It looked like a
typical Austrian intellectual's home. That office was as
memorable as the conversation we had there.

I had grown up with Freud's teachings and understood them well. We associated with many young ana-
lysts. This was not the first time I had met Anna and
Sigmund Freud, but it was my first personal interview
with them and the first time I had been alone with them.

Freud was very well traveled, especially, like my
own family, in Italy, and he knew everything about art.
He opened the door for me. He was extremely well
mannered, a real gentleman with a certain European
politeness that you can't put into words.

He had a European education where a certain
amount of knowledge was part of your growing up. He
was as well versed in art and art history, as he was in
psychoanalysis. In his work he always referred to people
like Michelangelo and the culture of his time. It was a
period in Europe filled with intellectual development.

So, there was Freud—the classic picture of him—
smoking his pipe, his little white dog at his side. He was
an old man then, already sick and suffering from a rare
form of cancer of the jaw. Anna, who was tall and had
grey eyes, never seemed to care much about her appear-
ance. She wore a dress that even at that time seemed
very old-fashioned. Even so, she was quite impressive to
me and yet very kind.

As a young girl, I was quite in awe of these two
international figures, but both she and Freud made me
feel comfortable right away. They asked me questions

116

about my knowledge of analysis and apparently I satisfied them. They agreed to make an exception and allow me to study with them.

I consider this initial meeting with Anna and Sigmund Freud as the core moment of my career—I really don't know if I would have pursued my path in the manner that I did without that meeting.

This course in child analysis never took place. The next day, on March 12, 1938, the Nazis summoned Anna Freud and treated her quite badly. With the help of the international community, she and her Father escaped to England. Our family was scheduled to leave at the same time.

My departure from Vienna to Prague, where my family was on vacation, was equally sudden. George and I would write each other through intermediaries, but earlier in March when he learned about the election news, he telephoned me. We were both shocked when the call went through, as we hadn't dared talk by phone before this. George instructed me to be prepared to leave at a moment's notice.

It was my Godmother, Pauline, who arranged for my travels. Before I left she gave me a beautiful gold bracelet, which I treasured until it was lost some years later. There were a number of people we knew who had fled before me, but I managed to get on the last train they allowed to cross the Austrian border.

About thirty people were picking me up at the train station, all friends of my Mother. I didn't know it then, but I could have been killed on the journey on the train, so they were all excited to see that I came through safely. In fact, while I was on the train, it was stopped and those who were Jewish-looking were arrested. Since I had auburn hair and blue eyes, they bypassed me. I had no idea that the Anschluss[34] was happening and that the

Nazis had invaded Austria until after I arrived.

At the station there were two men. I overheard one of them say, "Annemarie looks just like her Mother." The other man replied, "I don't look think she looks like her because her Mother is so beautiful." In the moment when I should have been filled with joy at escaping the Nazis, this is what stuck in my memory. Since then I have often been told this story isn't true, but that is my strong recollection of it.

In Prague, I met a whole society of educated people that my Mother had grown up with. When our vacation was over, our family and one of their students went back to Switzerland by car, circling around Germany by driving through Hungary, Yugoslavia and Italy. Some of the borders were very rigid—at one we had to get undressed as they checked through everything.

We realized that we couldn't stay in Switzerland forever because the Swiss would not let you immigrate, so we began making all the arrangements for relocating to America. Harald Baruschke made it possible for us to get our American visas, which were more and more difficult to obtain with so many immigrants trying to get out of the country.

In order to get our visas, we had to travel to Zurich, so my parents, my younger brother and sister and George and I set out to do so. Fortunately, George was able to persuade the authorities not to put a "J" for "Juden" or Jew stamped on our passports. We had a little adventure at that time. George had all of our passports in his hand and put them on top of the car before he got into drive, and forgot them there. As soon as he'd gone for a few minutes he remembered them, but by that time they were all over the street. I have always felt that we've been under some kind of protection, because we found them all. If they had been lost, our whole future would have been different.

We continued to live in Switzerland, running the boarding school at Les Rayons because we needed an income, until it was time to go. It was actually in the French-speaking part of Switzerland, but none of us except my Mother were that fluent in their spoken French. We all knew English pretty well, so that became our primary language.

The Quakers also played a part in helping us in our attempt to flee. There was a Quaker woman who was a student at my parents' school and somehow realized that we needed the money to emigrate. Also, you couldn't go to America without a sponsor to guarantee you, and so the novelist Thomas Mann[35] and the journalist Dorothy Thompson[36] became our sponsors. Dorothy Canfield Fisher[37] may also have played a role. I only remember this vaguely, but it was a very important part of our ability to leave the country.

Once we had our passage to America secured, we needed to begin to plan what our future would be like. We had done everything to make it possible to get to America but; remember, we were leaving for an unknown country. At this point, our adventures really started. It was a very daring thing to do. My Father's policythemia was getting worse. On top of it, he was in a deepening depression because he didn't want to leave Germany. Entering the country was in itself was a risky thing, as we were not sure they would admit him.

George sailed to America on the ocean liner the "S.S. Georgic" on a round-trip ticket, to make it look like a pleasure trip. He was eligible for the draft in Germany and they wouldn't let him go if he didn't have a return ticket. He departed from Le Havre, France and arrived in New York City on November 6, 1938. Once there, he began to look for some property so that we could start a school. Our immediate family followed six months later, in April of 1939, with the exception of Hanns and Edith, who arrived a year later. In contrast to George, who sailed under rather luxurious circumstancees, we came across the ocean in a small merchant cargo boat holding two dozen passengers. It was a very rough trip spanning two weeks to get across the ocean and I was very seasick. We were very frightened because we had no idea where we were going or whether we would sink in the middle of the ocean.

Gertrud Bondy
Emigration Papers

Max Bondy
Emigration Papers

Early one morning, we were all called on deck. There she was, rising out of the mist—the Statue of Liberty, just as we'd imagined her. I think we all felt the most unbelievable sense of relief to arrive in New York. Seeing the statue was really an event. Somehow it meant that our ordeal was over, that we were really free of the Nazis and that we were safe.

Fortunately, we did not land at Ellis Island. I don't believe they would have let my Father, with his illness, into the country. This may have been arranged through some relatives that George had in New York, one of whom was a private investigator. Even so, we were so overwhelmed we could hardly experience it. Along with the relief was enormous anxiety. It was more than I could bear. It was the exactly the feeling I had when we left Marienau. I felt that leaving and moving to another country was so powerful emotionally, that I didn't have the strength to really embrace it.

Annemarie Bondy
Emigration Papers

Despite the excitement of finally standing on American soil, I felt so totally German and I still do.

We seemed a million miles from Marienau, the place that was my home, where I belonged. My Mother was much more flexible and a citizen of the world. She adapted well. But my Father never really survived it. He was a broken man. In contrast to my siblings, I was just old enough to experience it all and yet still too young to really cope with it. I don't think I've ever coped with it. It destroyed something in me and there is still a deep hole in me that will never be filled.

I barely remember exiting the boat. Suddenly, it seemed, we were on the sidewalk, sitting on our suitcases. We waited for what seemed an eternity. George had somehow overslept and was four hours late in picking us up, but I don't remember being angry with him for it. We were all ecstatic to see one another.

It was all like a dream. I was about to turn twenty-one and not a child anymore. I was numb from my experiences, but inwardly I cried tears of joy when I saw George's face.

CHAPTER FOURTEEN
A New Life

Passport Photo, 1939

Press Portrait, 1958

Our trials were not over, of course. The first thing we did in the U.S. was to find some clothes for my brother Heinz. The custom in Germany was for little boys to wear short pants called "knickerbockers" and the children in America made fun of him. We truly had no money, but somehow felt we had to buy him something appropriate to wear. We put them in the car, the only luxury we had, and they were stolen right away. I don't remember what we did after that.

The second thing we did was to try and find a school for Heinz. We found boarding a school that turned out to be horrible—it was a school in Connecticut—so we took him out of it very quickly.

It was a very tense time. George, who had been in the U.S. for six months, had met up with some relatives who turned out to be Nazis. I remember feeling that it was just too much for this to happen just after we'd gotten through immigration, but we had to be nice to them, because they might be able to help us.

Just after our arrival, we got a telegram saying that my Mother's brother, Jula, had killed himself. No one, not even my Father, wanted to tell my Mother. I was the one who finally had to do it and fortunately she accepted it. She somehow had the intuition that it would happen.

It was a strange time to think about getting married, but George and I felt this was the right thing to do. We had originally wanted to get married in Switzerland in a really sweet little chapel but found out the Swiss were following the German rule and would not allow a Jewish girl and an Aryan man to marry. So we had to postpone our wedding.

So, two weeks after our arrival in New York, on April 20, 1939 (ironically, Hitler's birthday), George and I officially became husband and wife. The wedding was kind of a funny story. We went to find a Justice of the Peace to marry us. We were wandering around the streets of New York when we got to a courthouse where they were having a trial. The doorman said, "If you give me some money, I'll get you in." So they disrupted the trial and stuck a book in front of the judge and he read the formalities. I didn't quite understand what was going on, but finally the judge said, "Kiss the bride," and everyone clapped, then the trial continued. The people in the audience, who were rather seedy looking, were the same people who were going through the trial. Perhaps because of all the confusion, the judge forgot to date the marriage certificate. We had to go back the next day to have him do this and our wedding date was listed as April 21 instead of April 20.

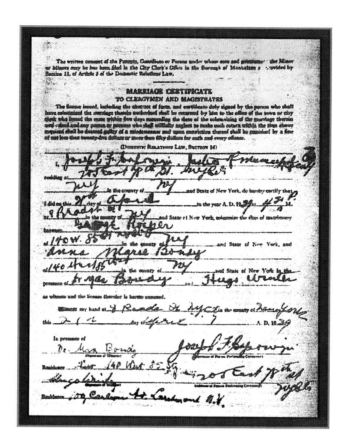

Marriage Certificate
Annemarie and George Roeper

My wedding was somewhat Spartan. I don't remember carrying flowers and I'm sure I didn't wear a hat, but sadly I never got to wear the white wedding gown that we had made in Germany. It was a beautiful dress! All of our clothes and most of our possessions had been in a big box that was nailed closed that they wouldn't release at the border because we didn't have the money for the duty. But we did have the wedding rings[38] that George had purchased in Switzerland. Later, I found some of my Father's books, but not my beautiful dress, at a sale on the side of road.

After the ceremony, we then went to our tiny little apartment. I think it was in a hotel that we lived, and that's where my Mother had arranged for dinner. It was very intimate—just my brother, my sister, my parents and George and I. We were the smallest wedding party you've ever seen. Our honeymoon consisted of taking my brother to boarding school in Connecticut.

The one luxury my Mother thought we should have was a nice wedding meal. She knew that George liked oysters, so we had them that night for dinner. Whatever we ate that evening we must have been ordered, because my Mother didn't cook. We had some champagne, but I imagine no more than one bottle. You have to imagine that we had very little then. During the wedding night, George got very ill and vomited the entire time. There was no way of fulfilling the marriage promise that evening!

George and Annemarie, 1940

A few years later, my brother Heinz volunteered for the American Army (this was one way to speed up naturalization) and he became a U.S. citizen in 1943. He had very hard training as he was in intelligence. For years I wrote to him every day. When we were young we were very close. Because he was so much younger, George and I became surrogate parents for him. He was with us constantly and he loved George dearly.

Heinz Bondy

Soon after we came to America we began a summer camp in New Hampshire with thirty children. This became Windsor Mountain School in Windsor, Vermont in 1940 and shortly afterwards it moved to Manchester. The school year in Manchester started with only fourteen students, but grew quickly enough to allow us to move to a larger campus, in Lenox, Massachusetts in 1944. My Father taught classes in Latin, but the primary responsibility the school fell on Heinz's shoulders. He officially became Headmaster in 1951.

In 1940, both my parents were granted their citizenship, perhaps because they were running a school.

Windsor Mountain School

**Christmas Gathering
at Windsor Mountain School**

It took Ulla and I until 1945 to receive our papers, and George's papers were approved one year later. He had found a gun in the attic of the house we were renting and naively tried to turn this in to the authorities. Because he was considered an "enemy alien," not a refugee as I was, his citizenship was delayed.

That year my Father suddenly decided he had to go back to Germany. He was so homesick. He took what little money that we had to make the trip and tried to reclaim Marienau under the German reparations policy. By then he had become a U.S. citizen and in part this caused his request to be denied. He finally gave up and he was very bitter about this for the rest of his life.

At that time, we had many immigrants from all over the world at the school. We had a number of

English students whose parents had sent them to us so they would avoid the Blitz. My Father tried to work with them a little bit; but for the rest of his life my Father lived with us as a shadow of his former self. His disease was progressing and he finally came to a hospital in Boston. Ulla's husband, Dr. Don Gerard, was a well-known physician in that hospital and he tried to help my Father. There were great efforts to keep him alive with blood transfusions, but he had lost his interest in living.

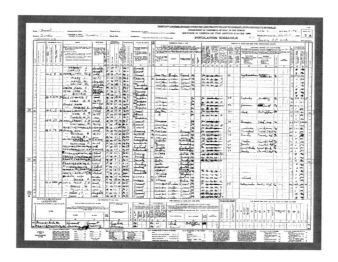

**1940 U.S. Federal Census Report
for Max, Gertrud and Heinz Bondy**

He died in on April 13, 1951. He was only fifty-eight years old.

My Mother would survive him by twenty-six years until her own death on April 30, 1977 in Detroit, but she lived to see their work thrive through The Windsor Mountain School and in the City and Country School, the sister school that George and I began in Michigan in 1941. This evolved into what is now The Roeper School,[39] and is still prospering.

131

Hill House
The Roeper School, 1946

Children Exit Hill House
The Roeper School

When I lived under the Nazis, I somehow came away with the feeling that there was nothing to be done about this world. In America, I felt so strongly that we had a second chance. It was our desire to educate children in a way that we thought would really improve this world and bring out the best in them. We did this with all the ideas that we were able to import from Marienau and successfully create something like it here.

As our philosophy evolved, its principles became known as S.A.I. or Self Actualization and Interdependence. It was our intent to create an educational atmosphere that would insure that what happened in Nazi Germany would never occur again. This has been my life's work and I am deeply indebted to my parents and to Sigmund and Anna Freud for providing the basis for this work to be done.

The Roeper School continues to be very unique and it has maintained an idealistic point of view, which expresses itself in its strong sense of community and the way parents, students and teachers interact. The amazing thing is that although we have had many different leaders, the basic philosophy of the school has been carried on by the students. This has been a source of great satisfaction to me.

George and I ran The Roeper School until his retirement in 1979 and my own retirement in 1980. At that time, I began consulting with gifted parents and children and I developed my own method of evaluating children known as "Q.A." or The Annemarie Roeper Method of Qualitative Assessment®, as a more expansive alternative to the I.Q. test.

George and I enjoyed a marriage as rich and culturally diverse as our life as educators. We raised three children together and continued to evolve our creative vision of early childhood education until George's death on August 24, 1992. At the time of this writing, I have three grandchildren and three great-grandchildren. When I think of what might have happened, the fact that my family has not only survived but also flourished here in America is a great comfort to me.

George and Annemarie   **Gertrud and Max**

As I depart this existence, at age 93, I want to express my love for my family, my friends and for all the children who have been such an important part of my life. It all began what seems like so many years ago in the once-idyllic land of my girlhood.

I can still see so clearly the purple heather, the golden fields, the shimmering woods and water. I can feel the warmth of the autumn sun and beneath my feet, the familiar road to my home at Marienau.

It is there that my heart, my soul and my most treasured dreams will always belong.

Annemarie Roeper died
on May 11, 2012
in Oakland, California.

Marienau still exists
following many of the principles
begun by the Bondy family.

Annemarie in 1951

Annemarie in 2011

Tributes:
In Memoriam
By Heinz Bondy

As Annemarie's younger brother, I have probably known Annemarie longer than any of you. Our early youth was spent in Germany and we left Germany together. I think for her it was much more difficult than it was for me to leave what she regarded as her home.

In this country, it was clear to me that Annemarie was not an accidental educator. She was a born educator from a family of educators. It was a tradition in our family. My parents were educators. My wife and I were educators and one of my sons is the head of a school in Pennsylvania, so the tradition carries on.

Leaving our home and coming to a new country with a new language brought Annemarie and I closer together. We were both interested in education and I spent thirty-five years in education and she did also. My first job in America was here at The Roeper School, which was then called the City and Country School. I can always remember that when I went to George to ask him how to be a good teacher, he said, "Start class at 9:00 in the morning and let them out at 2:00." This is advice that I have followed all my life. Annemarie taught at the Windsor Mountain School for a year and then opened the school here. I guess I was one of the first teachers, but I learned a great deal from them and it has been a pleasure for me to come back here and see all the many friends of the school and admirers of Annemarie.

As I said, I probably knew Annemarie better and longer than most of you. We argued occasionally— about education and about life in general—but in the end, we were very close and I shall miss her greatly.

Annemarie Roeper
Early 1960s

Tributes:
A Few Thoughts
on This Memoir
By Tom Roeper, Ph.D.
Professor of Linguistics
University of Massachusetts

One can hear my Mother's voice in this memoir. Karen Mireau has a perfect ear for her eloquence and adds her own literary grace. It enables us to connect her words to her love of books and the world they create — like an engraving of her childhood emotions. It is gratifying that we can share the voice of our Mother through this memoir with her larger family and the larger world she cared about. It is, of course, a memoir, not a history, many details may have been distorted by time, but they are alive as memories nonetheless.

Decades of animated family conversation never showed me, with such poignance, how her imagination and emotions rose and sank together in childhood. One can sense how she reaches out to an earlier self, and used those memories to reach out to each new child she saw, utterly individually, until her very last days. Her Mother, Gertrud Bondy, gave her a reservoir of self-respect that she drew on until she died, but yet she says it was "not a happy childhood" because she felt quite different from other children. Typically, she talks about the good part of her temper tantrums: they were an assertion of a child's right to some power in her life. Her story gives us all a little inspiration, a sense of how we can helpfully weave our own experiences into the lives of our children—yet it is the child's life: no one can guarantee happiness.

At first the larger forces surrounding her school

world in Marienau are only dim quiet shadows, which, as she describes, turn suddenly into a political tornado, vastly beyond what a young woman can bear. She said a few months ago that she knew of no book that described what it was like for a teenager to experience Nazism, so she set out to do it. Like many teenagers now—including many at the Roeper School—one can see in her a kind of pure fury at injustice from which adults can always learn.

Her descriptions of living in a school rekindled my memories of living at the Hill House at the Roeper School when I was four to seven years old. Since it was a day school, I experienced the children arriving suddenly, and then a huge empty house when they left. It was my home, and yet it was shared with so many people to whom it was also a kind of home. It was how my brother, sister, and I grew up.

As in Marienau, we lived in a precious world, entirely designed by our parents, with few glimpses of the outside. I remember outside school interactions made me shiver at first. A policeman, a store clerk, random adults in Birmingham Michigan, spoke to me and all the children with an authoritarian edge that I never felt either at home or at school. And the same occurred in my first venture to a two-week summer camp at Cranbrook when I was nine. The adults spoke in a different way to children, and I cried the first three days for reasons that were not clear.

The children at Roeper now share this world too. A story about the school (where I had the pleasure to work in 1979) comes to mind. A teacher told everyone a tale about herself and a fourteen-year-old student. When she first came to the school, she asked the student to "report to the main office," and the student simply said to her "at this school, you can just ask me to go to the

140

main office, 'report' is not a Roeper word." Of course, the real story here is that the teacher could cheerfully explain how she was learning from the student about what underlies the atmosphere at the school.

The vision of the human being that George and Annemarie held proceeds both from a commitment to community and from Freudian psychology. It was really an advance view of the revolution in psychology in the 1950s. The behaviorist "stimulus-response" approach championed by behaviorism was inherently authoritarian. It was replaced in the "cognitive revolution" with a recognition that only infinitely creative algorithms— mathematically represented by "recursion"—could capture mental ability.

My parents admired Jerry Bruner who, following Noam Chomsky, extended the notion of inherent creativity from language (which is what I study) to education. Creativity characterizes all human beings every moment. Each sentence we say represents a unique thought and a unique emotion. Chomsky extended the notion of unconscious emotions to the claim that there are unconscious ideas—that most of our thinking lies beyond our view. A fundamental consequence—which I think is the heart of the Roeper philosophy is this: if much of mental life is unconscious and individual, then we must respect the deeper psychology of every child because we can never quite know it. Each child's perspectives and opinions are inevitably unique.

Until her last days, she was eager to have philosophical conversations about life, school, and the brain. It was hard to feel unhappy about imminent death in her presence because it seemed she was still aimed at the future. One of my last conversations with her this year dealt with this topic. I recounted an email exchange I had with Noam Chomsky, who articulated his debt to

Freud, but he and I both felt that Freud had been unclear how unconscious the unconscious was. After a long discussion, she said to me, "No, the unconscious is not completely unreachable." If it were, we could never have integrity because our unconscious might be doing the opposite of our conscious. No, she said, we must build a world where we feel in touch and at ease with our unconscious selves—where through introspection and a supportive environment we can learn to find out what creates a sense of harmony in our whole personality. This is why holistic thinking has a home that fits the most sophisticated form of cognitive psychology.

It is important to assert: we each have the freedom to choose who we want to be and no one has the right to saddle us with labels we disavow. A current example is perhaps apt: the Jewish community of Amherst sponsored a wonderful Palestinian teenager and college student. I asked him one day what it was like to be a Muslim in Amherst and he responded, "Well, actually I recently became a Buddhist" so he wasn't a Muslim anymore. Of course, that is his right and just the kind of personal freedom that the Bondy/Roeper philosophy espoused. It makes perfect sense that one should want to define oneself and ally oneself as one chooses— it is not a choice that others, or history, dictates. Max Bondy and his Father, who both allied themselves with artists and intellectuals, had every right to decline a particular religious label, and had no desire to be labeled Jewish. At the end of the book my Mother declares that she feels "German," but to me she is simply herself, the complex kind of individual she celebrated.

These themes can be found in the Morning-Talks that Max Bondy gave that she mentions and my Father often fondly recalled. Oddly, some of those connections would make us laugh now. While he loved modern dance, Max felt that jazz somehow undermined personal integrity (or something like that), while now we can look at jazz as a quintessential illustration of spontaneous creativity that unites mental, emotional, and physical dexterity where we sense the unconscious roots of our conscious actions. All of that "Bach in the morning" that my Mother says here that she loved must have biased her Father against jazz. I guess we can even be creative in generating intolerance!

Beyond this memoir, the Marienau School needs to be linked to the history of Reformpädagogik [Progressive Education]—which is currently being revived in a number of interesting schools in Germany. While I am far from an expert on the topic, I'd like to provide a little background. Prior to the Landschulheimbewegung [Boarding School Movement], there were traditions coming from Norway that emphasized handicrafts and the Wandervogel ["wanderbirds"], which emphasized hiking, that fed into the Youth Movement that originated before WWI. Educators Hermann Lietz, Kurt Hahn, the Gehaabs and the Waldorf Schools provided some educational institutions that advocated co-education, handicrafts, farming, and the dignity of manual labor. Max Bondy participated in several of the early meetings of the nascent Youth Movement, which drew several thousand people. These schools and the movement were profoundly anti-Victorian in spirit. After WWI, a fresh wind blew. The Young Socialists in the Socialist movement, cultural innovations in the Weimar republic, and psychoanalysis were intellectual currents that had various sorts of impact on these schools.

In rough terms, the Bondy school, founded in 1920 was at the forefront, probably unique, in fashioning a visionary combination of these three ideas. First, how to structure a community was a core topic among the

Young Socialists—Curt Bondy wrote his dissertation on the topic. Second, psychoanalysis, through my Grandmother, placed the inner life, friendship, deep conversations, and an awareness of the unconscious as a positive source of creativity as a pedagogical value. It was an extremely important departure from the emphasis on pathology that emerged from Freudian psychology. And finally, cultural openness, including a welcome attitude toward modern dance, abstract art, and avant-garde theatre, and curiosity about what was happening in America.

Other schools were really quite different: their emphasis often lay on farm work, manual labor as a response to emotional problems, fairly strict curricula built around handicrafts, and distrust of wild experimental cultural innovation that did not proceed from German tradition. The English variety of progressive education, glorified in the book *Summerhill*, championed absolute freedom that our parents felt was both superficial and undermined the deeper vision of humanity that they held. In both the Bondy and Roeper schools, the seriousness of responsibility, group and individual, was an ever-present ingredient in the recognition of individuality. The commitment to community was expressed through the idea that teachers and students could be friends, call each other by their first names, live in the same buildings. Students at Marienau participated in the admission process and (I learned from this memoir) helped choose the farm on which Marienau was built. Democracy was really at the core of community decisions.

Ideas from progressive education have influenced every school to some degree. Those directly descended from the European tradition in the U.S. are legion. One can draw direct connections, person by person, to the

144

Upland Hills School in Michigan, Putney School in Vermont, Shady Hill School in Cambridge, the Common School in Amherst, the Little School of Seattle, the Colorado Rocky Mountain School—and many, many others where the details are not known to me.

And yet the American schools also come in different flavors. Dewey's ideas of "learning by doing," the role of arts, farm life, ecology, diversity and civil rights have been seen as more important than community structures and introspection. It is my strong suspicion that the particular blend of progressive ideas found at the Roeper and Bondy schools remains distinctively unique.

Annemarie Roeper's voice in this book must be added to her other voices. Most of her writing provides engrossing stories about children she has known and how she spoke to them. In this book, she allows us to see her as one of those children—so she herself becomes the last child to benefit from her wisdom.

And as I write this, I can almost feel her nodding in approval (mostly), and together with many of the readers of this memoir, she will remain a humane conscious and unconscious force in our imaginations.

Annemarie, 1991

Tributes:
"Wow"
By Peter Roeper
Public Health Researcher

Someone once told me that Annemarie Roeper was huge. I looked at my Mother, looking rather delicate in her leather chair, and thought, 'She is really small, physically small.' But I had an inkling of what that person meant.

My Mother was a large, complicated, formidable personality—a robust being, a force. She was, as they say, an experience. She left a mark on all who encountered her, a mark that in nearly every case caused one to think, to understand, to grow and, often, to smile. She was a unique, powerful soul in many people's lives.

Annemarie Roeper was kind of unstoppable—creating a school, seeing clients, writing books and articles until the end. My Mother was large enough in personality and effect, and lived long enough to inhabit and fill several different worlds. She made the world more interesting, richer, more fun and one that I certainly felt privileged to be part of.

Perhaps the most appropriate way to describe Annemarie Roeper is as an educator, one who liked to think about children and how they saw the world and what kind of learning would most effectively meet their needs. Her greatest and most important creation was The Roeper School in Michigan, which she developed with her husband George, but she deserves the title of educator not just because of this. To interact with her was to be inspired and to learn. She would totally accept you as you are and she would make you think, wonder, consider new concepts, to ask, to doubt, and to reconsider. Her view of the world was not confined by how it was supposed to be but as unlimited as her potent mind could make it. She did not see a simple world. This is what an educator does and this is the effect she had.

After their experience in Nazi Germany, my parents very much wanted to create a place where people could live together harmoniously, where respect would dominate relationships, and where power, particularly arbitrary, angry power would not play a role. In their school nothing was ever done from fiat alone but required explanation, thought, understanding, and dialogue. She and my Father wanted to see if it was possible to make a school to match their ethics and views on children, which had their origin at Marienau, the school founded in Germany by Annemarie's parents. They made it happen . . . it worked, and it continues to work.

My Mother's ethics were not just a prescription of how people were supposed to be but included a full awareness and acceptance of human emotions, with all their vagaries. They were an active and powerful part of who she was. Her ethics were very much based on decency and justice, but decency and justice as it applies to people's psychology. You might say her ethics applied to the soul.

I wrote a list of descriptive words about my Mother and the list became long. Many of the words in this list were opposites. She had many conflicting qualities and one way to understand her was through the terms yin and yang, where each side defines the other side and one side does not exist without the other.

She could be buoyant and charming and she could be desperate and needy. She could be creative and imaginative, pessimistic and optimistic, a dreamer and a realist. She had strong left-wing progressive views, and

148

thought everyone was equally worthwhile, and she was also spoiled and aristocratic. She was well educated and unschooled. She was confident and despairing. She was very naïve and very sophisticated. Like a magnet she pulled you towards her and could also push you away. Whatever she felt, she expressed very fervently. Her enthusiasm could be exhilarating; her personal despair could be overwhelming.

This dynamic combination became captivating, entertaining, enthralling, and certainly surprising. She liked to laugh and I personally loved to make her laugh or see a wry expression come across her face to become a gleaming smile. She never told a joke or used pat phrases. She made you laugh with her cleverness. She knew she was clever, but she was so good at it she never seemed to be showing off. She knew how to lighten a situation with humor. And you never, ever knew when she might say something funny and delightful that would be totally disarming. You were always impressed with the spontaneous mind that was the source. Her intelligence could light the room.

What my Mother taught us was that we are all human, all complex. We are full of contrary actions and feelings, forces working against each other and with each other to create turmoil and beauty, misunderstandings and humor. That is what it is to be human. And that is what my Mother was. She was not a perfect person, perfection being a concept that she would reject as absurd.

To know Annemarie Roeper was to be very impressed, perhaps a little overwhelmed, maybe stunned, or mesmerized, or astonished, maybe bemused, or perhaps to just think, 'Wow!'

And who does not love 'Wow?' As her son, I thank her for what she contributed to all of our lives . . . and I will miss her.

Tributes:
Completing the Circle
By Karen Roeper
Founder, Essential Motion®

This memoir was born of my Mother's deep desire to give future generations a sense of our family's roots and history. At the time of her death she had three children, three grandchildren and three great-grandchildren. In her last years she mentioned repeatedly how significant it was to her that there were three generations of her family born in the U.S. It meant to her that the family was now clearly and safely rooted in America.

Being forced to uproot and leave her mother country due to the Nazis was the major trauma of her life. The fact that her family escaped and safely arrived in New York Harbor in 1939 was one of the major wonders of her life. As the generations grew in the U.S., and as she aged, Annemarie expressed an increasing urgency that these and future generations have a clear image of the family history. She also felt it important to give them a larger historical perspective. She wanted to share her experience growing up in the unique environment of her parents' boarding schools, and to paint a picture of life in the early 20th century—pre-television and before computers, automobiles and telephones.

Annemarie was an incessant thinker and had an amazingly creative mind. She was inspiring and provocative. She left a great legacy reflecting her brilliance and tenacity. The Roeper School is one example, of course, as well as her many articles and books on gifted education, and in particular her insights into the emotional life of gifted children and adults.

Creative thinking permeated her life—from the

fanciful stories she told me as a child to the creation of the school itself, and the innovation of the "open classroom" approach. One example I personally cherish is when we both lost our homes and all our possessions in the Oakland fire in 1991. After that tragic event, which was another huge and devastating loss, she wrote me a series of vignettes to make up for the lost photographs of my childhood. They were entitled "Photographic Memories of Karen as Stored in Her Mother's Heart."

My Mother was also a great listener. When she ran her school, she had an open door policy for the students and the teachers. They knew they could come and talk to her whenever the need arose. Whoever crossed my Mother's path was affected by her presence. She had the gift of helping people recognize and value themselves at a very deep level.

As her daughter, I had the same experience of her openness and availability. She was always interested and curious about everything I was doing. As an adult, I had the opportunity to work with my Mother and Father at The Roeper School. When she moved to California, she got very interested in the transformational movement work, Essential Motion®, that I was developing and she participated in my courses.

My Mother had a brilliant mind and craved stimulation. She was a voracious reader and had many ongoing e-mail correspondences. Her intellect and her need to express and create was vital right up to the end of her life. In her last month she was obsessed with neuro-science. She was deeply impressed by the research on brain plasticity and kept saying, "I have to keep living so I can learn about the brain."

I was always struck by my Mother's desire to understand and to know herself better. She was open and honest about herself and how she experienced life, and she had a deep need to express herself. This memoir is indeed a reflection of that curiosity, a part of her own introspective learning process, as well as a story she wanted to share with others.

Community and family were the mainstays of Annemarie's life. In her last years her greatest joy was being with her children, grandchildren, great grandchildren and extended family. She loved having all four generations gathered together for a celebration.

I am eternally grateful for my Mother's gifts of love, laughter, playfulness, creativity and above all her curiosity. This memoir is Annemarie's final loving gift to all of her family, her worldwide community and to all future generations.

> *"When you love, you complete a circle.*
> *When you die, the circle remains."*

- John Squadra

Annemarie, Age 89

BONDY/ROEPER TIMELINE

The following dates and descriptions are based on source documents and anecdotal material provided by family and friends of Annemarie Roeper.

They are intended to provide a general historical context for Annemarie's recollections. Any errors or omissions are purely unintentional.

Please contact Azalea Art Press with any additions or corrections.

1861	Abraham Lincoln becomes the 16th U.S. President
1868	November 13 George Paul Röper (George Alexander Roeper's Father) born in the city of Lubeck, Germany. The higher-status spelling of the name Roeper, using an 'e' instead of an umlaut, was adopted later in the 19th century.
1870	Franco-Prussian War
1871	German Empire merges all German states, with the exception of Austria. Otto von Bismarck becomes Chancellor of Germany.
1875	Birth of novelist Thomas Mann.

1879	Thomas Edison demonstrates the first incandescent light bulb in New York.
	June 10 Anna Meyer (George Roeper's Mother) born in Swatow, China.
1881	January 16 Paul Lauer born to David and Katerina Lauer. (Mathilde "Matti" Wiener's future husband.)
1884	First electromechanical television system patented by Paul Nipkow, a 23-year-old German university student.
1885	First "motorwagen" built by Karl Benz in Mannheim, Germany.
1886	December 17 Mathilde ("Matti") Wiener born to Gustav and Olga Wiener in Prague, Czechoslovakia. (Annemarie's maternal Aunt.)
1887/8	Julius "Jula" Wiener born to Olga Lauer and Gustav Wiener. (Annemarie's maternal Uncle.)
1889	April 20 Birth of Adolf Hitler.
	October 7 Gertrud Wiener (Annemarie's Mother) born in Prague to Olga Lauer and Gustav Wiener.

1892   May 11
        Max Bondy (Annemarie's Father) born in
        Hamburg, Germany to Marie Lauer and
        Siegfried (Salomon) Bondy.

        Nikola Tesla demonstrates the trans-
        mission and radiation of radio frequency
        energy.

1893   March 22
        Cornelia "Nelly" Bondy born to Marie
        Lauer and Siegfried (Salomon) Bondy in
        Hamburg. (Annemarie's paternal Aunt.)

1894   April 3
        Twins Curt and Walter Bondy
        (Annemarie's paternal Uncles) born to
        Marie Lauer and Siegfried (Salomon)
        Bondy.

1901   Theodore Roosevelt becomes the 26th
        President of the United States.

1902   Herbert "Fritz" Bondy (Annemarie's
        paternal Uncle) born to Marie Lauer and
        Siegfried (Salomon) Bondy.

        First production-line manufacturing of
        automobiles by Ransom Olds in Lansing,
        Michigan.

1903   Orville Wright takes the first powered
        piloted flight in an aircraft invented by he
        and his brother Wilbur.

1905	February 20
	Johann ("Hanns") Ludwig Georg Roeper (Annemarie's future brother-in-law) born to George Paul Roeper and Anna Meyer Roeper.
	Mathilde "Matti" Wiener (Annemarie's maternal Aunt) marries Paul Lauer.
1907	"The Bondy House" residence is constructed in Hamburg for Siegfried (Salomon) Bondy by architects Hans and Oskar Gerson.
	Gustav Wiener (Gertrud Wiener's Father) dies. Gertrud and Olga Wiener move to Vienna, Austria.
	August 23
	George Gustav Lauer (Annemarie's maternal cousin) born to Mathilde ("Matti") and Paul Lauer.
1909	Annemarie's maternal Grandmother, Olga Wiener, remarries to Rudolf Feldmann.
1910	August
	Max Bondy graduates from Wilhelm High School in Hamburg.
	September 7
	George Alexander Roeper (Georg Alexander Hermann Roeper), (Annemarie's future husband) born to George Paul Roeper and Anna Meyer in Hamburg.

1910/11	Max Bondy studies law and economics at Munich University. He travels to Italy during the 1911 winter term to study art history.
1912	Max Bondy and Gertrud Wiener return to Italy along with a group of students chaperoned by Mathilde ("Matti") Bondy Lauer and her husband, Paul Lauer.
1912/13	Max Bondy studies art history and history at Freiburg University. He writes *Die Grundlagen der Freischaridee* (The Basics of a Fresh Idea), an article outlining his ideas for a progressive school, influenced by the German Youth Movement.
1914	July 28 WWI begins. Gertrud Wiener begins the study of medicine at the University of Vienna and psychoanalysis with Sigmund Freud. Max Bondy volunteers in WWI as an artillery officer.
1915	September 1 Edith Gertrud Marie Sowade (future wife of Hanns Roeper/Roper) born to August Sowade and Maria Sojka Sowade (1893-1955).

1916   September 30
Marriage of Max Bondy and Gertrud
Wiener.

Marie Lauer Bondy (Max Bondy's
Mother/Annemarie's paternal
Grandmother) dies.

Walter Bondy (Max Bondy's brother) is
killed in friendly fire in Romania.

1917   May 3
Thomas Gustav "Chum" Wiener (Winner),
(Annemarie's maternal cousin) born in
Prague to Julius "Jula" and Franciska
Wiener.

Max Bondy awarded the Hanseatenkreuz
(Hamburg Medal of Honor) for serving in
WWI.

1918   May 25
Peter Lauer (Annemarie's maternal cousin)
born to Mathilde ("Matti") Bondy and Paul
Lauer.

August 27
Birth of Annemarie Martha Bondy in
Vienna, Austria to Max and Gertrud
Bondy.

November 11
WWI ends.

1919	Max and Gertrud Bondy and their daughter, Annemarie, move to Erlangen, Germany.
	December 22 Max Bondy awarded a doctorate in art history from the University of Erlangen.
1919/20	Max and Gertrud Bondy found the "Freie Volkshochschule" (Free High School) in Bavaria with Harald Schultz-Hencke and Martha Paul-Hasselblatt.
1920	Gertrud Bondy awarded her medical doctorate from the University of Erlangen.
	May 26 Jan Gerhardt "Gerdi" Wiener (Annemarie's maternal cousin) born in Hamburg to Julius "Jula" and Franciska Wiener.
1920-23	Max and Gertrud Bondy found "Freie Schul und Werkgemeinschaft Sinntalhof" (Free School and Work Society Sintalhof) in Brückenau, with Ernst Putz.
1921	Gertrud Bondy studies with psychoanalyst Dr. Otto Rank.
	October 9 Ursula "Ulla" Babette Bondy (Annemarie's sister) born to Max and Gertrud Bondy in Brückenau, Germany.

July 29
Adolf Hitler becomes the leader of the
National Socialist (Nazi) Party.

1923   Autumn
Max and Gertrud Bondy part ways with
Ernst Putz and found "Schulgemeinde
Gandersheim" (School Community
Gandersheim).

1923   February 28
Birth of Donald Louis Gerard (future
husband of Ursula "Ulla" Bondy).

1924   The entire Bondy family is baptized as
Lutherans.

George A. Roeper arrives at School
Community Gandersheim at age 13.

June 2
Birth of Heinz Gustav Eric Bondy
(Annemarie's brother) to Max and Gertrud
Bondy in Gandersheim, Germany.

1925   July 18
Mein Kampf by Adolf Hitler published.

1926   Scottish inventor John Logie Baird gives
the world's first demonstration of a
working television system.

1928   Marienau, a 300-acre farm, is purchased by
Siegfried (Salomon) Bondy near Lüneberg,
Germany.

1929	Herbert Hoover becomes the 31st U.S. President.
	Easter Founding of the school at Marienau by Max and Gertrud Bondy.
	October 29 Stock market crashes on Wall Street in New York.
	George P. Roeper (George A. Roeper's Father) dies.
1930	George A. Roeper graduates from Marienau.
	Nazis become 2nd largest political party in Germany.
1932	Olga Wiener (Annemarie's maternal Grandmother) dies.
	Death of Siegfried (Salomon) Bondy (Max Bondy's Father/Annemarie's paternal Grandfather).
1933	Nazis first infiltrate Marienau and begin altering the curriculum. They will increasingly control the school for four years until it is officially turned over to Dr. Bernhard Knoop in 1937.

January 30
Adolf Hitler becomes Chancellor of
Germany.

February 27
German Reichstag burns.

March 12
Dachau, the first concentration camp,
opens outside Berlin, Germany.

Franklin D. Roosevelt becomes the 32nd
President of the U.S.

Curt Werner Bondy co-founds The Jewish
Center for Adult Education with Martin
Buber.

July 14
Nazi Party becomes Germany's only political party.

October 14
Germany quits League of Nations.

1934   August 19
        Adolf Hitler becomes Führer of Germany.

1935   Nuremburg Race Laws strip German Jews
        of rights.

        Anna Meyer Roeper (George A. Roeper's
        Mother) dies.

George A. Roeper receives his M.A. from the University of Berlin.

1936   May
Curt Werner Bondy and William B. Thalhimer establish Gross-Breesen near Breslau, Germany.

Gertrud Bondy establishes "Les Rayons" at a former Quaker school near Lake Geneva in Gland, Switzerland.

October 15
Hanns Roeper (George A. Roeper's older brother, Annemarie's brother-in-law) marries Edith Gertrud Marie Sowade.

1937   March
Annemarie Bondy graduates from Marienau.

April 2
Marienau is officially sold to Dr. Bernhard Knoop.

Immigration of Max and Annemarie Bondy to Gland, Switzerland.

Autumn
Annemarie Bondy begins the study of medicine at the University of Vienna. She interviews with and becomes the youngest protégé to be accepted by Sigmund and Anna Freud in Vienna for studies to begin in spring, 1938.

1938   November 12
                Operation of Jewish businesses prohibited
                by the Nazis.

                December 3
                Jews are officially required to sell property
                and possessions to the Third Reich at a
                fraction of their cost or risk punishment or
                confiscation.

                Hyde Park Farm is purchased by William B.
                Thalhimer in Virginia as a haven for Jewish
                émigrés from Gross-Breesen.

                Stephen Bondy (Annemarie's paternal
                cousin) is born to Herbert "Fritz" Bondy
                and third wife, Lilo Bondy.

                March 11
                Annemarie Bondy flees on the last train
                from Vienna to Prague, before the border is
                shut down and Hitler invades Austria.

                March 12/13
                The Anschluss. Austria is annexed into the
                German Third Reich.

                November 6
                George Roeper arrives on the "S.S.
                Georgic" in New York harbor.

                November 9
                Kristallnacht, "The Night of Broken Glass."

George G. Lauer (Annemarie's maternal cousin) marries Edith Kornfeld.

1939   April 3
Immigration of Max, Gertrud, Annemarie, Ursula and Heinz Bondy to New York.

Immigration of Curt Bondy to New York via Holland and Spain.

April 20
Annemarie Bondy and George Roeper marry in New York. The judge neglects to date their certificate and they return on April 21 to have it signed.

Summer
Max and Gertrud Bondy open a summer camp at Lake Winnipesaukee, New Hampshire.

Autumn
Max and Gertrud Bondy open their first school in the U.S., the Windsor Mountain School in Windsor, Vermont. George and Annemarie Roeper teach pre-school and elementary classes at Mt. Kemble School in Bernardsville, New Jersey.

September 2
Thomas "Chum" Wiener (Annemarie's maternal cousin) immigrates to New York. He changes his name to 'Winner.'

1940   January 8
Hanns and Edith Roper arrive in the U.S.
Hanns changes his Roeper surname to
eliminate the 'e'.

September 22
Windsor Mountain School moves to
Manchester, Vermont.

George and Annemarie Roeper return to
Vermont to work at Windsor Mountain
School. Enrollment is 14 students. George
Roeper is listed as Headmaster/Teacher,
Max Bondy as President/Teacher, Gertrud
Bondy as School Psychologist/Teacher and
Annemarie Roeper as Elementary and
Nursery School Teacher.

1941   Annemarie Roeper is invited to direct the
Editha Sterba Nursery School in Highland
Park, Michigan. George Roeper establishes
the Roeper Grade School in the same
building.

Heinz Bondy graduates from Windsor
Mountain School and enters Wagner College on Staten Island, New York on a full
scholarship.

Edith Sowade Roper and Clara Leiser cowrite and publish Skeleton of Justice with
E.P. Dutton.

Jews ordered by Nazis to wear yellow stars.

First use of gas chambers at Auschwitz concentration camp.

March 24
Cornelia "Nelly" Bondy (Annemarie's paternal Aunt) immigrates to the U.S. with her husband Manfred Israel Zadik (1887-1965).

April 6
Julius "Jula" Wiener commits suicide. (Annemarie's maternal cousin.)

December 7
Japanese bomb Pearl Harbor.

December 8
United States and Britain declare war on Japan.

December 11
Hitler declares war on the United States.

Gross-Breesen closes.

1942   Due to increasing enrollment, the Roeper Grade School and Editha Sterba Nursery School move to Detroit, Michigan.

Heinz Bondy forced to leave Wagner College as an "enemy alien" (the college on Staten Island overlooked the entry of New York harbor and the Brooklyn Naval Yards).

1943	Heinz Bondy enlists in the U.S. army and becomes a citizen at Camp Hale, Colorado. He trains in military intelligence at Camp Ritchie, Maryland.
	Jeanette (Jenny) "Puppi" Roper (Annemarie's niece) born to Hanns and Edith Roper.
	August 23 Thomas Walter Roeper born to George and Annemarie Roeper in Vermont.
1944	Windsor Mountain School moves to Lenox, Massachusetts.
	June 6 D-Day. Heinz Bondy lands on Omaha Beach in the invasion of Normandy, just a few days after his 20th birthday.
	July-December Heinz Bondy in the 79th infantry in the assault on Cherbourg, the liberation of Paris and the Battle of the Bulge.
1945	March-April Heinz Bondy, with the 79th infantry, crosses the Rhine to occupy the German Ruhr Valley and to liberate Dauchau.
	April 12 Harry S. Truman becomes the 33rd U.S. President.

April 30
Adolf Hitler commits suicide.

May 6
Teresienstadt concentration camp is
liberated.

May-December
Heinz Bondy works in the Allied occupa-
tion and military government of Germany
until deactivated in December.

May 7
Unconditional surrender of German forces
to Allies.

May 8
V-E Day.

July 16
First atomic bomb dropped on Hiroshima,
Japan.

August 9
Second atomic bomb dropped on Nagasaki,
Japan.

August 14
V-J Day. Japanese agree to unconditional
surrender.

The end of WWII.

November 20
Nuremberg war crimes trials begin.

Heinz Bondy returns from the war.

1946	Max Bondy tries to reclaim Marienau under the German reparations policy, but is finally denied, in part because he is a U.S. citizen.

George and Annemarie Roeper relocate their school outside the city to Bloomfield Hills, Michigan. It is renamed City and Country School of Bloomfield Hills with 90 students through 6th grade.

April 11
Peter John Roeper born to George and Annemarie Roeper.

1947	Ursula "Ulla" Bondy (Annemarie's maternal Aunt) weds Donald Louis Gerard (b. February 28, 1923) in New York City.

1948	Jan Gerhardt "Gerdi" Wiener (Annemarie's maternal cousin) sentenced to five years hard labor at Kladno steelworks in Czechoslovakia.

Gandhi is assassinated.

1949	March 1 Karen Marion Roeper born to George and Annemarie Roeper.

April 14
Kathleen Gerard (Annemarie's maternal niece) born to Ursula "Ulla" Bondy Gerard and Donald Louis Gerard.

Heinz Bondy graduates from Swarthmore College and obtains his M.A. from Bryn Mawr, then teaches at the City and Country School until 1951.

1950   Before he retires in 1959, Curt Bondy returns to Germany and becomes director and professor at the Psychologisches Institut of Hamburg University, one of the first Jews to be given an academic position after the war.

September 28
Charles Donald Gerard (Annemarie's maternal nephew) born to Ursula "Ulla" Bondy Gerard and Donald Louis Gerard.

President Truman sends military advisors to aid the French in Vietnam. Vietnam War begins.

1951   Heinz Bondy becomes Headmaster of Windsor Mountain School in Lenox, Massachusetts.

April 13
Max Bondy dies in Boston, Massachusetts.

Steven Lauer (Annemarie's maternal second cousin) born to Peter and Terry Lauer.

Color television introduced in the U.S.

1952	Nicholas Lauer (Annemarie's maternal second cousin) born to George G. Lauer and Edith Kornfeld Lauer.
1953	Birth of Martha Ellen Harnly (future wife of Peter Roeper).
	Dwight D. Eisenhower becomes the 34th U.S. President.
1955	City and Country School becomes the first private school in Michigan to be racially integrated. (The school employed an African-American teacher beginning in 1942.)
	Timothy Lauer (Annemarie's maternal second cousin) born to George G. Lauer and Edith Kornfeld Lauer.
	June 8 Philip Walter Gerard (Annemarie's maternal nephew) born to Ursula "Ulla" Bondy Gerard and Donald Louis Gerard.
1956	City and Country School becomes the second elementary school in the U.S. to be designated as a school for gifted children.
1961	John F. Kennedy becomes President of the U.S.
1962	Lieutenant John H. Glenn, Jr. becomes the first American to orbit the Earth.

1963	August 28 Dr. Martin Luther King, Jr. delivers his "I Have a Dream" speech. John F. Kennedy assassinated in Dallas Texas. Lyndon B. Johnson becomes 36th U.S. President.
1964	Jan Gerhardt "Gerdi" Wiener (Annemarie's cousin) emigrates from Czechoslovakia to the United States. Jan Gerhardt "Gerdi" Wiener marries his third wife, Zuzana. They raise two children, Tanya and Joseph. The Beatles appear on The Ed Sullivan Show.
1965	Annemarie Roeper consults with Joan Ganz Cooney, Maurice Sendak and others on the concept and development of "The Way to Sesame Street."
1966	The name of City and Country School changes to Roeper City and Country School in honor of the school's 25th anniversary.
1968	April 6 Dr. Martin Luther King, Jr. assassinated in Memphis, Tennessee. June 6 Robert Kennedy assassinated in Los Angeles, California.

1969	Dr. Bernhard Knoop retires as head of Marienau School and is succeeded by Dr. Gunter Fischer.
	January 20 Richard M. Nixon elected 37th U.S. President
	July 20 Apollo 11 astronauts take man's first walk on the moon.
	Premiere of "The Way to Sesame Street."
1970	December 31 Death of Ursula "Ulla" Bondy Gerard (Annemarie's maternal Aunt.)
1971	June 22 Karen Roeper marries Tom Carman.
1972	Death of Herbert "Fritz" Bondy (Annemarie's paternal Uncle.)
	President Richard M. Nixon visits China.
1973	September 22 Tom Roeper weds Laura Holland.
1974	August Nixon resigns. Gerald Ford becomes U.S. President.
1975	Windsor Mountain School closes due to financial difficulties.

1976	Death of Curt Werner Bondy (Annemarie's paternal Uncle).
	End of Vietnam War. Election of National Assembly paves way for reunification of North and South Vietnam.
1977	Jimmy Carter becomes 39th U.S. President.
	December 18 Jamey Carman (Annemarie and George Roeper's grandson) born to Karen Roeper and Tom Carman.
	April 30 Death of Gertrud Bondy (Annemarie's Mother) in Detroit, Michigan.
	Charles Donald Gerard (Annemarie's maternal nephew) marries Dr. Judith Weinstock. They have one son, Adriel, and a daughter, Eva.
1978	Spring George and Annemarie Roeper awarded honorary doctorates from Eastern Michigan University and establish The Roeper Review, a quarterly professional journal.
	August Death of Cornelia "Nelly" Bondy (Annemarie's paternal Aunt) in California.

February 16
Maria Ann Roeper (Annemarie and George Roeper's granddaughter) born to Tom Roeper and Laura Holland.

September 4
Birth of Amy Elizabeth Dickinson (future bride of Jamey Carman).

1979   George Roeper retires at the end of the school year.

1980   Annemarie Roeper retires.

        John Lennon assassinated in New York City.

1981   January 20
        Ronald Reagan inaugurated as U.S. President.

1983   U.S. admits shielding former Nazi Gestapo chief Klaus Barbie, 69, the "butcher of Lyon," wanted in France for war crimes.

        Edith Kornfeld Lauer (wife of George Lauer, Annemarie's maternal cousin) dies.

1985   May 26
        Death of Edith Sowade Roper (Hanns Roper's wife, Annemarie's sister-in-law).

August 25
Birth of Timothy Abraham Roeper
(Annemarie and George Roeper's grandson)
to Tom Roeper and Laura Holland.

Philip Walter Gerard (Annemarie's maternal
nephew) marries Sherry Frazer. They have
one son, Isaac, born in 1990.

1986   Wolf-Dieter Hasenclever becomes Head-
        master at Marienau School under the motto
        "ecological humanism" signaling a return to
        the philosophical roots of Max and Gertrud
        Bondy.

        Austrian president Kurt Waldheim's service
        as a Nazi army officer revealed.

1988   October 14
        Death of Hanns Roper (Annemarie's
        brother-in-law.)

1989   George H. W. Bush becomes U.S.
        President.

        Fall of the Berlin Wall.

1990   The Bondy House is built in Hamburg,
        Germany to house the archives of the
        Bondy legacy and other resources.

        South Africa frees Nelson Mandela after a
        27½-year imprisonment.

1992   August 24
George Roeper dies in Oakland, California.
His memorial on September 20th is attended
by nearly 800 people.

Autumn
A ceremony is held at The Bondy House in
Hamburg, Germany (where the archives are
held) for the 100th anniversary of Max
Bondy's birth.

1993   The name of the Roeper City and Country
School is changed to The Roeper School.

Bill Clinton becomes 42nd U.S. President.

1999   Annemarie Roeper is the first recipient of
the President's Award from the NAGC
(National Association for Gifted Children)
for a lifetime of distinguished service.

2001   George W. Bush assumes the U.S. Presi-
dency.

2003   October 25
Karen Roeper marries Peter Rosselli.

2004   April 20
Death of Thomas Winner (Annemarie's
maternal cousin) in Cambridge, Massachusetts.

2005	August 13 Maria Ann Roeper (Annemarie's granddaughter) weds Frederico Santos Azcarate.
2006	October 8 Marriage of Peter Roeper to Martha Ellen Harnly.
	November 3 Danilo Roeper Azcarate (Annemarie and George Roeper's great-grandson) born to Maria Ann Roeper and Frederico Azcarate.
2008	Annemarie Roeper is the first to be videotaped for the NAGC's Legacy Series.
2009	January 5 Alexander Holland Azcarate (Annemarie and George Roeper's great-grandson) born to Maria Ann Roeper and Frederico Azcarate.
	Barack Obama becomes the 44th U.S. President and the first African-American to hold that office.
2010	October 15 Jeanette "Puppi" Roper (Annemarie's niece) weds Joseph Gordon Moore (b. March 28, 1943).
	November 26 Death of Jan Gerhardt ("Gerdi") Wiener (Anne-marie's maternal cousin) in Prague.

2011   Maia Joëlle Carman (Annemarie and George Roeper's great-granddaughter) born to Jamey and Amy Carman.

2012   May 11
Annemarie Roeper dies in Oakland, California.

June 16
A memorial for Annemarie Roeper is held in Muir Beach, California.

August 25
A memorial for Annemarie Roeper is held at The Roeper School in Bloomfield Hills, Michigan.

November 16
The NAGC honors Annemarie Roeper with a tribute in Denver, Colorado.

TEXT NOTES

[1] Olga Lauer Wiener was one of four children born to Moritz Lauer and Julie Goldmann, including Bertha, Marie (who later married Annemarie's paternal Grandfather, Siegfried Bondy) and Emmy. They were not related to David Lauer, who married Katerina Bondy, her paternal Grandfather's sister.

[2] Gustav Wiener, born in 1807, had three sisters: Clara, Mathilde and Johanna.

[3] Rudolf Feldmann later died in Teresienstadt concentration camp.

[4] Julius "Jula" Wiener committed suicide in 1941. He and his second wife, Margaret, who was not Jewish, lived in Yugoslavia. He knew he was going to be taken to a concentration camp the next day and so they decided to kill themselves before that would happen. He asked his son Jan Gerhardt "Gerdi" Wiener, whether he wanted to kill himself with him. Gerdi declined. After Jula and his wife took the poison pill, they knew they would die a few hours later. Gerdi and his Father sat down and played a game of chess until Gerdi realized that the time had come and then fled to Czechoslovakia.

[5] When Ulla grew up, she became a social worker in America, working with unmarried mothers. She married Dr. Donald Gerard and had three children: Kathleen "Kay" (1949), Charles (1950), and Philip (1955).

[6] Heinz trained in intelligence and served in the U.S. army, experiencing many of the critical moments of World War II. He became Headmaster of the Windsor

Mountain School in Lenox, Massachusetts in 1951. He adopted two sons, Peter and Eric. He is now married to Carolyn Louks.

[7] Siegfried (Salomon) Bondy was the son of Leopold and his wife, Anna, who owned a bakery in the German town of Bohemia. He was a banker and investor who became a multi-millionaire and funded the schools created by Max and Gertrud Bondy.

[8] Cornelia "Nelly" Bondy married Manfred Zadik from Poland. She later married Walter Thompson. She had three children: Frank Zadik, Walter Thompson, and Michael Thompson.

[9] Herbert "Fritz" Bondy (1902-1972) became a chemist. Curt (1894-1992) became a noted psychologist and social educator. Walter died during friendly fire in WWI and Max Bondy died of polycythemia in 1951.

[10] The Gerson brothers, Hans (1881-1931) and Oskar (1886-1966) built one of Hamburg's first skyscrapers, the Ballin House. They later settled and built homes in northern California. Their younger brother Ernst Gerson (b. 1890) died in 1984. One of his daughters, the artist Elizabeth Kavalagh, lives in Berkeley, California.

[11] Jan Gerhardt "Gerdi" Wiener, cousin of Annemarie Bondy Roeper, died in Prague on November 26, 2010 at age 90. His Father, Julius "Jula" Wiener committed suicide with his second wife in 1941 to avoid being arrested by the Nazis. Gerdi fled and served as a RAF radio navigator in WWII. Gerdi's birth Mother, Franciska, died in 1942 in Teresienstadt concentration camp. In 1945 he returned to Czechoslovakia. When the

communists took over in 1948, he did hard labor at Kladno steelworks for five years. He immigrated to the U.S. and by 1964 became a professor at American University. Two Holocaust documentary films were made about him: *Čtyři páry bot* (*Four Pairs of Shoes*) in 1997 and *Fighter* in 2000. He also wrote two books: Assassination of Heydrich and Always Against the Tide: a Jewish Survival Fate of Prague 1939-1950 with Erhard R. Wiehn, as well as an oral history of his experiences in WWII, Reminiscences of Jan G. Wiener, that resides at Columbia University. Gerdi had two sons from his first marriage and two children, Tanya and Joseph, from his third marriage to Zuzana.

[12] Thomas Gustav Winner was the eldest son of Julius "Jula" Wiener and maternal first cousin to Annemarie Roeper. Thomas was a noted scholar, activist and expert on Russian literature. He spoke 20 languages and after graduating from Harvard, he taught at Columbia, Duke, University of Michigan and Brown, where he established the first American semiotics center. He married Irene Portis and they had two children: Ellen and Lucy. Upon his death in 2004, he had two grandchildren, Benjamin and Kyla.

[13] Peter Lauer, Annemarie's maternal cousin, was born in 1918, married twice and had a son, Steven Strauss, and a daughter, Linda.

[14] Annemarie's maternal cousin, George Lauer, and his wife, Edith Kornfeld, were turned back from immigrating to England due to a miscommunication and ended up being sent in 1943 to Theresienstadt concentration camp until the Russians liberated them on May 5, 1945. They survived because George was an expert in chem-

istry and supervised the rat extermination and delousing. Edith who was a social worker, cared for children at Theresienstadt. They were later responsible for helping transport 300 children to northern England and later immigrated to America where George became a successful research chemist. They had two sons—Nicholas (b. 1952) and Timothy (b. 1955). Nicholas married Linda Poole in 1984. Their son, David Lauer (b. 1989) graduated from The Roeper School in 2008. Timothy married Suzanne Monson in 1979. They have three children: Emilie, Hazel and Samuel.

[15] Curt Werner Bondy held a Ph.D. in Philosophy from Hamburg University and became a full professor at Göttingen University in 1925. Later, he was a professor at William and Mary College in Virginia and in 1950 became director and professor at the Psychologisches Institut of Hamburg University.

[16] In addition to Jews, 5 million people were murdered by the Nazis among groups targeted for persecution— Poles, Roma (Gypsies), Soviet POWs, the mentally ill and physically handicapped, Jehovah's Witnesses, and homosexuals. Homosexuality was considered a mental illness. Some were institutionalized and many others were sent to concentration camps.

[17] Martin Buber was a prolific Israeli philosopher, essayist and translator whose ideas on education; particularly his emphasis on dialogue, community and individual growth, profoundly influenced the development of Marienau.

[18] William B. Thalhimer, who co-founded Gross-Breesen with Curt Bondy, later became the national chairman of

the Refugee Resettlement Committee of the National Coordinating Committee (NCC), the umbrella organization for Jewish immigration to the United States.

[19] From: <u>My Personal History</u> by Gertrud Bondy, a brochure printed at Windsor Mountain School, Lenox Massachusetts, 1970, and presented to Gertrud by her students.

[20] When George and Annemarie integrated the Country and City School in the 1950s, it was, to the best of their knowledge, the first private school in the state to be racially integrated.

[21] Adi Schlesinger, one of Annemarie's best childhood friends, and his wife, Ina Schlesinger, had a daughter, Anne, and two sons: Stephen and Richard.

[22] The town of Lüneburg was the center of the salt trade from the 12th century to 1980. It was spared during the war, which preserved its medieval character. It is home to two large salt baths. Lüneburg later hosted the Belson trial against the perpetrators of crimes at Auschwitz and Bergen-Belson concentration camps. It also was the site where the leader of the S.S., Heinrich Himmler, committed suicide and is buried.

[23] The Depression in Germany (1930-1935) was fueled by the stock market crash in the U.S. in 1929 and reached crisis level in Germany in 1931 due to the reparations Germany was made to pay after the Treaty of Versailles. The currency became hyperinflated. This played an important role in Hitler's seizure of power in 1933 and the rise of the Nazi party, which promised and implemented economic recovery by 1935.

[24] From: <u>A Testament of the Survivors, A Memorial To The Dead: The Collection of Gross-Breesen Letters and Related Material</u>.

[25] The "race-shame" laws in Nazi Germany were based, in part, on how black people were treated in America and on laws enacted by legislatures in the American South.

[26] The Warburgs were among the wealthiest investment bankers and philanthropists in Europe. The architects Hans and Oskar Gerson, who built "The Bondy House" residence, also built one of their villas.

[27] George Roeper's Father, George Paul Röper, was born in 1868 and died in 1929. His Mother, Anna, was born in 1879 in Swatow, China and passed away in 1935. The spelling of the name Roeper, using an 'e' instead of an umlaut, was considered a higher status spelling and adopted later in the 19th century.

[28] George Roeper's older brother Hanns married Edith Gertrud Marie Sowade in 1925. Hanns changed his name from Roeper to Roper upon coming to the U.S. in 1940, as he thought it was pretentious to use their altered surname. They had one daughter, Jeanette (Jenny) "Puppi" Roper, born in 1943.

[29] George and Annemarie Roeper were each awarded an honorary doctorate degree from Eastern Michigan University in 1978.

[30] View an excerpt of Edith Roper's story at www. questia.com/library/book/skeleton-of-justice-by-clara-leiser-edith-roper.jsp.

[31] On November 9-10, 1938, over 7000 Jewish shops were looted and 267 synagogues burned down by Nazi S.A. ("Sturm Abteilung" or storm troopers.) An estimated 91 Jews were killed and another 30,000 incarcerated in concentration camps during Kristallnacht or "Night of Broken Glass."

[32] Dr. Bernhard Knoop, a member of the National Socialist Party, was approved by the Nazis to take over the administration of Marienau in 1937 and marked a change to a more conservative curriculum. Despite his own political affiliations, Dr. Knoop was married to Angelika Probst and then to Anneliese Graf, both of who had family ties to The White Rose Society and the German resistance. Dr. Knoop was Headmaster of Marienau for 32 years. He was succeeded by Dr. Gunter Fischer in 1969. In 1986, Wolf-Dieter Hasenclever assumed management of the school under the motto "ecological humanism" signaling a return to concepts derived from the Germany Youth Movement and first instituted by Max and Gertrud Bondy.

[33] While Annemarie was a teacher at Les Rayons she met a student, Angelica Eisenstadt, who later reunited with her in Berkeley, California and became a life-long, trusted friend.

[34] Hitler's invasion of Austria on March 12, 1938 and its annexation on March 13, is known as "The Anschluss."

[35] German writer, philanthropist and Nobel Prize laureate Thomas Mann (1875-1955) fled Nazi Germany in 1933, eventually immigrating to the U.S. in 1939.

³⁶ Dorothy Thompson (1893-1961), "The First Lady of American Journalism" was the first American journalist expelled from Nazi Germany. She was one of the few female radio news commentators of the 1930s.

³⁷ Author, educator and social activist Dorothy Canfield Fisher (1879-1958) worked with Maria Montessori and was responsible for introducing the Montessori educational method to the United States. She became a lifelong supporter of the Bondy/Roeper schools and philosophies.

³⁸ There is a German custom that when one spouse dies, the surviving spouse fuses both rings together. This is the one that Annemarie wore after George's death until her own passing.

³⁹ The history of the evolution of The Roeper School and its philosophy can be accessed at www.roeper.org.

ANNOTATED BIBLIOGRAPHY

This informal collection of source documents, books and resources is intended as a starting point for exploring the complex history and legacy of the Bondy/Roeper family.

Assassination of Heydrich
Jan Gerhardt Wiener
Grossman Publishers, 1969.
Jan Wiener's telling of the Czech resistance movement's role in the death of S.S. chief Reinhard Heydrich, known as 'The Butcher of Prague' on May 27, 1942 is interspersed with personal recollections of his experiences in Czechoslovakia.

Die Architekten Brüder Gerson.
Mit Einer Einleitung von Werner Hegemann
(The Architect Brothers Gerson. With an introduction by Werner Hegemann.)
Friedrich Ernst Hübsch, 1928.
An illustrated survey of the work of German architects Oskar and Hans Gerson.

George C. Lauer:
Story of My Life and Times,
Written in 1993-1994
Self-published memoir by George Gustav Lauer, cousin of Annemarie Roeper.

Gertrud und Max Bondy: Wegbereiter der modernen Erlebnispädoagogik?
(Gertrud and Max Bondy: Pioneers of Modern Experiential Education)
Barbara Kersken

Verlag Klaus Neubauer, 1991.
Print edition of a lecture by Barbara Kersken on the concept of experiential education, which had its origins in the German Youth Movement.

Immer gegen den Strom: ein jüdisches Überlebensschicksal aus Prag 1939-1950 (Against the Tide: a Jewish Survival in Prague, 1939-1950)
Jan G. Wiener, Erhard R. Wiehn
Hartung-Gorre, 1992.
Jan G. Wiener's account of his experiences in WWII as told to Erhard R. Wiehn.

Life and Work of the Hanseat and Reform Pedagogue Max Bondy (1892-1952) in Pictures and Documents
Hamburg, October 1999 / Marienau School
An exhibition catalog in tandem with the opening of Marienau School's archives. The 8 1/4" x 11 3/4" perfect-bound catalog is in German and English.

Max und Gertrud Bondy in Marienau: Die Geschichte einer verdrangten Padagogik
(Max and Gertrud Bondy in Marienau:
The History of a Suppressed Pedagogy)
Barbara Kersken, 2012.
Book by Marienau School archivist, Barbara Kersken, on the roots and history of the Bondy legacy.

Normalcy and Pathology in Childhood: Assessment of Development
Anna Freud
International Universities Press, 1965.

Cited by Annemarie Roeper as the text that became the basis of her own work with children.

The Pity of It All:
A Portrait of the German-Jewish Epoch, 1743-1933
Amos Elon
Metropolitan Books/Henry Holt & Co.
Historian Amos Elon portrays the panoply of factors leading to the enthusiastic assimilation of German Jews into their host country and the bitter irony of the anti-Semitism that resulted from pursuing their cultural ideals.

Reminiscences of Jan G. Wiener
Jan Gerhardt Wiener
Columbia University Library.
Unpublished oral history manuscript of Jan Gerhardt Wiener's experiences in WWII.

Report of the Ecole, "Les Rayons"
Community report from Les Rayons, Gland, Switzerland, 1938.

Skeleton of Justice
Clara Leiser and Edith Roper
E.P. Dutton, 1941.
See excerpts from the text at:
www.questia.com/library/book/skeleton-of-justice-by-clara-leiser-edith-roper.jsp.
Edith Sowade Roper served as a court correspondent under The Third Reich. In 1940, she courageously smuggled her notes exposing of the German legal system to America, where she completed and published her manuscript with co-author Clara Leiser.

Reformpädagogik heute:
Wege der Erziehung zum ökologischen
Humanismus: Marienauer Symposion zum 100.
Geburtstag von Max Bondy
(Progressive Education Today: Ways of Education for
Ecological Humanism: Marienau Symposium to Mark
the 100th Birthday of Max Bondy)
Wolf-Dieter Hasenclever
Lang, 1993.
Conference publication for the 100ᵗʰ Birthday of Max Bondy.

The Virginia Plan:
William B. Thalhimer and a Rescue
from Nazi Germany
Robert H. Gillette
The History Press, 2011.
An accounting of the heroic efforts of William B. Thalhimer to
help Jewish students emigrate from Gross-Breesen agricultural
farm in Germany to Virginia in America.

194

PUBLICATIONS
By Gertrud and Max Bondy

Speeches –
Max and Gertrud Bondy
Booklet presented to Gertrud Bondy from the Student
Body at Windsor Mountain School,
Lenox, Massachusetts, 1965.
The Bondy Collection, The Roeper School Archives,
Bloomfield Hills, Michigan.
Collection of speeches by Max and Gertrud Bondy given to the
students and faculty of Windsor Mountain School.

Gertrud Bondy:

Pädagogik und Psychoanalyse
(Pedagogy and Psychoanalysis)
Gertrud Bondy, Wolf-Dieter Hasenclever
Lang, 1990.

A Personal History
The Bondy Collection / The Roeper School Archives,
Bloomfield Hills, Michigan.
To learn more: archives.info@roeper.org.
Gertrud Bondy recounts the origins and histories of the alternative
schools founded by herself and Max Bondy. From a brochure
printed at Windsor Mountain School, Lenox, Massachusetts,
1970.

Über die Beeinflussung der blutbildenden Organe
durch kolloides Eisen, Terpentinöl und Abrin
(About the Influence of the Blood-forming Organs by
Colloidal Iron, Turpentine and Abrin)
Dissertation by Gertrud Bondy, University of Erlangen, 1920.

Max Bondy:

Baiersdorf, eine kunstgeschichtliche Untersuchung
(Baiersdorf: An Art Historical Investigation)
Dissertation by Max Bondy, University of Erlangen,
1919

Das neue weltbild in der erziehung
(The New World View in Education)
E. Diederichs, 1922.

Die grundlagen der freischaridee
(The Basics of a Fresh Idea)
1912/13.
Article outlining Max Bondy's views of progressive education.

Ich muß mich dann immer damit beschäftigen, bis ich es Euch gesagt habe" : Reden an junge Deutsche (1926-1947) Dokumente zu ihrem Verständnis, Kommentar, Anhang
("I Must Always Deal With it Until I Have Told You"
Speeches to Young Germans, 1926-1947).
Documents for their Understanding, Comments, Notes
Published by students at Marienau School, 1998.

Morning-Talks
Dr. Max Bondy
Schulgemeinde auf Gut Marienau,
May 1936.
Translated by Harald Baruschke, Cologne
and F. J. Gemmell,
B.A. Thornton Heath/Surrey
A 38-page 6"x9" booklet of Morning-Talks by Max Bondy to
the students of Marienau held over a 10-year period. Five of these
were addressed to children to age 15, the remainder to elder

196

children and teachers. Chapter titles include: On Bravery; A Talk to Confirmands; Dissipated; Our Formative Faculty; Birthday Speech, 1927; On Modern Dancing; The New Humanism; A Task for the "Landerziehungsheime"; Morning-Talk, February 1936; and Morning-Talk.

Annemarie, 1975

BOOKS, INTERVIEWS
& LECTURES
By Annemarie Roeper

Books:

Annemarie Roeper:
Selected Writings and Speeches
Linda Kreger Silverman, Ph.D. (Editor),
Richard Medeiros (Editor)
Free Spirit Press, 1995.
Articles and speeches by Annemarie Roeper spanning her professional life to 1995. A foreword by Linda Kreger Silverman, Ph.D., Director of the Gifted Development Center in Denver, Colorado, provides an insightful overview of the essence of Annemarie Roeper's life and philosophy.

Beyond Old Age:
Essays on Living and Dying
Azalea Art Press, 2011.
This provocative look at the universal challenges of aging explores Annemarie Roeper's unique view of what it is like to be "beyond old."

Children's Books:
Azalea Art Press, 2010.
Inspired by the children at The Roeper School, these timeless photo-illustrated books address the concerns of young readers. Available in trade paperback and hardcover reissues of the 1963 editions.

I Need All My Teddy Bears
Every new adventure also requires the security of holding onto the familiar.

The Plane Went Down in Buffalo
The experience of independence can sometimes contain an unexpected twist.

Small & Tall
Growing up is something every child wonders about.

Who Started It?
Conflicts are a healthy part of the process of growing up.

**Find Azalea Art Press titles at
http://www.lulu.com
(search by Annemarie Roeper or by title)**

**Educating Children for Life:
The Modern Learning Community**
Royal Fireworks Press, reprint 1990.
Using examples from her career as an educator, Annemarie Roeper creates a compelling blueprint for educating young people to become self-actualized and part of a global community.

**The "I" of the Beholder:
A Guided Journey to the Essence of a Child**
Great Potential Press, 2007.
The educational approaches, personal philosophy and development of the Annemarie Roeper Qualitative Assessment Method® are explored in this essential text for anyone interested in the education of gifted children.

**Living with Intensity:
Understanding the Sensitivity, Excitability, and Emotional Development of Gifted Children, Adolescents, and Adults**

Susan Daniels, Ph.D., Editor,
Michael M. Piechowski, Ph.D., Editor
Great Potential Press, 2009.
*Provocative essays on strategies for understanding and nurturing
sensitivity and creativity in gifted children and adults by
Annemarie Roeper and other scholars in the field of gifted
education.*

My Life Experiences
With Children:
Selected Writings and Speeches
Great Potential Press, 2007.
*Annemarie Roeper reflects on her journey as an educator,
innovator, school administrator and world citizen in this collection
of stimulating articles, essays and addresses.*

Interviews:

The European Lives of George
and Annemarie Roeper
*Unpublished first-hand interviews with Annemarie and George
Roeper by Pam Blair, Ph.D., an intimate friend of the Roeper
family. ©1992, Pam Blair.*

Holocaust Oral History Project: Interview with
Annemarie Roeper, San Francisco, California, 1992.
*Transcripts of taped interviews with Annemarie Roeper by Sylvia
Proean and Jake Birnberg.*

Interview of Annemarie Roeper
by Leila Evelev, Librarian of the Roeper School.
*Interviews conducted in Annemarie's home in Franklin,
Michigan. The Bondy Collection / The Roeper School Archives,
Bloomfield Hills, Michigan. Visit: archives.info@roeper.org.
Transcripts of the following 3 tapes:*

Tape 1 / October 28, 1978.
Tape 2 / November 4, 1976.
Tape 3 / November 11, 1976.

Roeper History: European Roots / Connections with History

The Bondy Collection, The Roeper School Archives, Bloomfield Hills, Michigan. Unpublished document by Marcia Ruff, Historian for The Roeper School.

A comprehensive summary of the European history of Annemarie and George Roeper by Marcia Ruff based on archival documents and direct interviews and correspondence with Annemarie Roeper.

A View From the Self: A Life History of Annemarie Roeper

Dissertation by Michele M. Kane, Ed.D. Chicago, IL 2006.

A lively, in-depth inquiry into the life and work of Annemarie Roeper and the development of the philosophy of The Roeper School drawn from years of intimate conversations with Annemarie Roeper.

Lectures:

The following four lectures by Annemarie Roeper can be accessed at: The Bondy Collection / The Roeper School Archives / Bloomfield Hills, Michigan. Visit: archives.info@roeper.org.

Annemarie Roeper / Lecture #1: "The History and Philosophy of The Roeper School"

Delivered by Annemarie Roeper at The Roeper School, October 10, 1995.

Annemarie Roeper / Lecture #2:
"First Encounter Between the Inner and Outer Worlds: A Child is Born; A Self is Born"
Delivered by Annemarie Roeper at The Roeper School, October 17, 1995.

Annemarie Roeper / Lecture #3:
"The Growing Self Encounters Relationship: School and Society"
Delivered by Annemarie Roeper at The Roeper School, October 24, 1995.

Annemarie Roeper / Lecture #4:
"The Role of Parents, Educators and the School Community"
Delivered by Annemarie Roeper at The Roeper School, October 30, 1995.

Marienau School
Winter View, Front Entrance

FILM/VIDEO RESOURCES

Across Time & Space
Kathryn Golden
Producer and Director
Searchlight Films, 2002.
www.searchlightfilms.org.
A sensitive, moving portrayal of the lives and educational legacy of the Bondy/Roeper family.
See excerpts of the film at:
http://www.youtube.com/user/searchlight1210.
Order copies by contacting searchlightfilms@me.com.

**An Evening
with Annemarie Roeper /
Portraits in Gifted Education:
The Legacy Series**
National Association for Gifted Children, 2008.
www.NAGC.org.
As the first to be honored in NAGC's Legacy Series, this video chronicle of Dr. Annemarie Roeper's educational theories is rich in personal experience and insight.
Order copies of the video at: https://www.nagc.org/nagc2/ngcShopper/ProdList_Result.aspx.

Fighter
Amir Bar-Lev
Producer and Director
First Run Features, 1999.
Two friends, Jan Gerhardt Wiener and Arnost Lustig, ponder the elusiveness of memory and truth in this 90-minute Holocaust survival documentary.
Copies of the film are available at:
http://www.barnesandnoble.com/w/dvd-fighter-arnost-lustig/4172478.

Four Pairs of Shoes (*Čtyři páry bot*)
Director: Pavel Štingl, CZ, 1997.
The story of Jan Wiener's adventurous escape from Nazi-occupied Czechoslovakia. After serving in the Royal Air Force, Jan Wiener was persecuted by the Communists and later immigrated to the U.S., where he became a professor at American University.

ONLINE RESOURCES

Annemarie Roeper's web page
http://roeperconsultationservice.blogspot.com.

Azalea Art Press
http://azaleaartpress.blogspot.com.
Azalea Art Press publishes innovative authors who inspire others to discover and manifest their creative potential.

Gifted Development Center
http://www.gifteddevelopment.com.
A resource center for developmentally advanced children and their parents providing in-depth assessment and counseling as well as a wide range of resources for families.

Great Potential Press
http://www.greatpotentialpress.com.
Books by Annemarie Roeper, Ed.D. and others providing core information for gifted children and parents.

Gross-Breesen:
A Testament of the Survivors,
A Memorial To The Dead
The Collection of Gross-Breesen Letters
and Related Material.
http://grossbreesensilesia.com/pdfs/1.pdf.
Chronicle of the life and letters relating to Curt Bondy and the development of the agricultural training farm at Gross-Breesen in Germany.

Marienau School (Schule Marienau)
http://www.marienau.com.de
Home page for Marienau School.
To write Marienau School:
Schule Marienau, 21368 Dahlem, Germany.

National Association
for Gifted Children
http://www.NAGC.org.
NAGC home page.

The Roeper School
http://www.roeper.org.
Home page for The Roeper School.

Royal Fireworks Press
http://www.rfwp.com
Writings by Annemarie Roeper, Ed.D. and other books for gifted children.

Searchlight Films
www.searchlightfilms.org
To view excerpts from the 'Across Space and Time' documentary of the Bondy/Roeper family, visit:
http://www.youtube.com/user/searchlight1210.
Order copies at: searchlightfilms@me.com.

Skeleton of Justice
www.questia.com/library/book/
skeleton-of-justice-by-clara-leiser-edith-roper.jsp.
Excerpts from the book by Edith Roper and Clara Leiser, published in 1941 by E.P. Dutton.

A Teen Holocaust Story /
Unitarian Universalist Association
http://archive.uua.org/re/faithworks/fall03/curriculum
andlearningresourcese.html.
The personal experience of George Landecker, a student at Gross-Breesen, by Frank E. Robertson.

The Virginia Plan:
William B. Thalhimer
and a Rescue from Nazi Germany
http://www.vahistorical.org/news/
lectures_gillette.htm.
Online lecture by author Robert H. Gillette about the emigration of students from Gross-Breesen to America.

Annemarie Roeper
An Ageless 92

PHOTO INDEX

Marienau School, 2010

FLOWERS IN THE SNOW

In Memoriam
Annemarie Roeper

By Karen Mireau

The horizon
was brilliantly blue that day:
the clouds all ice and ash
pinned like grey flowers
to the frozen Michigan sky

Spring seemed but a fairytale
of ancient woods and heathered hills
and waterways where she once drifted
hour upon hour in her wooden canoe
dreaming of "The Mystery"

Floating down the river
that led far, far away from Marienau
from the crush and tramp of Nazi boots
the terror that had shattered
her near-perfect childhood

When the time came, her family fled—
two fevered weeks by cargo ship
across the sea to New York harbor
and there began
to build the world anew

Their schools prospered and grew
and she woke again each day
to the laughter of students
who knew little of broken dreams:
of friends and family who would never return

That winter, when the snow rose
in darkening barricades
the children again grew restless for the sun
and from the long-buried country
of her innocence, something woke

She becalmed them, saying
"What about this . . . or this?"
then they all went out
and where there were none
painted imaginary flowers in the snow

She knew then
that she had purpose of her own
the power to heal and to inspire
and that she might do
some real and lasting good

Her forget-me-not-blue eyes
like a clear heaven
that gave and gave again
with utmost tenderness
the gifts of love and acceptance and truth

That was, and is,
and will always be our Annemarie

And any poetry left unsung
will echo in the voices of all those children
and the memory of
that beautiful kaleidescope
of winter flowers

Long after her time, and ours
has come and gone

ACKNOWLEDGEMENTS

I am deeply grateful to the Roeper Family—Tom, Peter and Karen—as well as their spouses, children and grandchildren, who have all contributed so generously to this fresh understanding of Annemarie's life and legacy.

Kay Whitney and Puppi Roper have been especially open and helpful in confirming anecdotal and genealogical details and I am so thankful to Heinz Bondy and his wife, Carolyn; as well as to Charles and Philip Gerard, for providing elements that added significant historical context to the story.

The work of Roeper family friend Pam Blair, who did extensive early interviewing with Annemarie and George, must receive special mention. Her exacting, intuitive recording of their life story has become one of the core references for anyone wishing to know more about the evolution of the Bondy/Roeper family.

A very special indebtedness must go to Marcia Ruff. On a personal level, her advice and support throughout this project have been invaluable to me. In her role as Historian for The Roeper School, her stellar research, writing and dedication to the organization of the literary and philosophical legacy of Annemarie and George Roeper will be indispensable to future students of the history of education.

My wholehearted thanks must also be given to Annemarie's dear friends Michele Kane and Linda Silverman, both of whom have been intimate confidantes of Annemarie's as well as excellent scholars of her literary life and work. Their writings have been instrumental in creating a well-rounded portrait of her contribution to gifted education.

I must also thank Annemarie's fine friends and colleagues Anne Beneventi, Susan Daniels, Ann Higgins and Joy Navan, as well as her editors and publishers Jim Delisle, Judy Galbraith and Jim Webb; all of whom have been instrumental in furthering our knowledge of the roots of Annemarie's global vision and the practical application of her philosophy.

There is no way to adequately express my admiration for Michael Piechowski's commitment to Annemarie's wellbeing and for his help in clarifying many of the meditations she had on her life. Their long and loving friendship, which included over a decade of daily emails, continues to be a source of inspiration to me.

I am also grateful for the on-going friendship and guidance of those in The Columbus Group, who have been such a dynamic part of Annemarie's intimate web of stimulating and mutually supportive women artists, writers, educators, healers and creative dreamers.

I would be remiss if I did not individually celebrate Betty Meckstroth, who as a very special friend of Annemarie's added much laughter and lively conversation to her days, as well as caring for her during times of crisis.

I am also indebted to Annemarie's companions— Angelica Eisenstadt, Ilse Hadda, Annetta Miller and Anita Navon—who have been steadfast touchstones of insight and wisdom for both Annemarie and myself. Ina Schlesinger also deserves praise for her friendship and unconditional support of Annemarie throughout her life both in Germany and America.

Kathryn Golden and Ashley James, co-founders of Searchlight Films, have contributed valuable and moving visual documentation of Marienau and Annemarie's life narrative through their film, 'Across Space and Time.' I am indebted to their research and their untold hours spent traveling with and interviewing Annemarie and her family.

My thanks also to Roselle Chartock, who was immensely helpful in sharing information from her upcoming book on Windsor Mountain School. Barbara Kersken, archivist at Marienau School has been a wonderful resource for photos of the early days of the school and provided much encouragement.

Great respect and appreciation must be accorded Dr. Nicola Hanchock, Marla Lay, Djuna Odegardand, Lois Peterson, Maia Russell and Inga Vanek, as well as Rosalie Lamb and all The Quirks—whose compassion and care were of immeasurable comfort to Annemarie, especially during her final days.

My deepest gratitude, of course, must go to Annemarie herself. As with all who knew her, from the very beginning our connection with her was a magical one. As she rejoins what she called "The Mystery," the depth and warmth of her expansive spirit and the feel of her gentle, reassuring hand upon ours will be greatly missed.

Karen Mireau
November 2012

To Order Books
or for more information, contact:

Karen Mireau
Publisher

azaleaartpress@gmail.com
http://azaleaartpress
.blogspot.com